I Am Underdog

# I Am Underdog

—ɯɯ—

## A Journey of Adversity & Blessings

#5 *(signature)* "Go Hoos"

Tony L. Covington

ISBN: 1546781900
ISBN 13: 9781546781905

# Dedication

This book is dedicated to my mother, Princetta Covington. May she Rest In Power. I still owe her a book of poetry. To my dad, Archie, thank you for sticking by me and being that positive influence, even when I didn't do things exactly the way you wanted me to do them. It's also dedicated to two of God's greatest gifts to me, my daughters Kennedy and Carter. You two are the best of me and I pray every day that God will place his hedge of protection around you. To my sister, Melanie, who has always been there as a confidant and best friend. She has always been more than just a sister and she has always known exactly when I needed her. To my close friends that have enhanced my life, especially those that have been there when they didn't have to be... you know who you are. And last but not least to my beautiful wife, Ericka. Thank you for sharing your life with me.

*Princetta Covington*

# Foreword

By Kennedy Covington

TONY COVINGTON: AN inspiration, a father, and an Underdog. I want to talk about my father's main trait; resilience. Tony Covington is a man that lives and breathes as a real-life example of resilience. It is represented quite adamantly throughout this book where my dad has always found a way to rise to the top. My father wrote this book in an attempt to remind all of the little dogs out there that it is okay to be little; it is all about accepting the fact that you are what you are and how to figure out where to go from there.

My dad has had his really high ups as well as really steep downs but when we talk about resilience, Tony Covington always finds a way to make it back and better. He has never been stuck in a bad place for long time due to his will to live, thrive, and be happy. My dad is an inspiration. Here and present in your hands is evidence of why he is one.

I remember a time when I told my dad that he was like a super-man to me. So, when I read this book, I was exposed to the Clark Kent side of my dad. I got to see my dad through a different lens.

So, when you read this book I hope that you take away some of the same things that I did. At the same time, I hope that you unveil something new and take away some new ideas that will help you to exhume that Underdog that has been there all along.

# Introduction

I AM UNDERDOG! I consider myself to be the eternal Underdog. An Underdog is defined as a person or team thought to have little chance of winning. All of my life I have been underestimated. People have frequently told me what I wasn't going to be able to accomplish or what I wasn't going to do. Sports have always played an important role in my life and when I was younger I was small in stature so maybe that's where the doubt or non-belief started. What these people never seemed to realize though, was that this dog may have been one of the smallest in the fight but the sheer amount of fight in this dog was tremendous. I have always relished my role as the Underdog and have taken great pleasure in proving the doubters and detractors wrong. When they said, "I was too small" in Pop Warner football, I proved them wrong. When they doubted me in high school and said that I was too small to play, I became one of the best players in the state of North Carolina. When they said that I wouldn't get a scholarship to a major college, I proved them wrong by earning a full athletic scholarship to the University of Virginia. Even then they said well he's a good student so his academics probably got him there. He will never play once he gets there. So, I took me, my 164 pounds soaking wet and a ton of belief in myself to the University of Virginia and excelled. I became a four-year starter, an all-conference player and an honorable mention All-American. Oh, and I earned my Bachelor's degree in four years. Then I heard that he is not good enough to go to the National Football League. He is too small and he's not good enough. I was selected in the fourth round of a twelve round NFL draft by the Tampa Bay Buccaneers. After all of that, I still heard the doubters rumbling in the weeds. He'll never make the team and besides Tampa Bay has had no history of success whatsoever. Even if he makes he will never play. I was in the starting lineup as a rookie and proceeded to earn All-Rookie honors leading all rookie safeties in tackles and interceptions. I went on to have a five-year NFL career. Not too bad for a guy who never stood a chance to make it in the first place.

It is amazing how people can question the ability of someone over and over again. What they never understood was that I had a belief in me that was bigger than life. No one handed me anything. I had confidence and a willingness to work harder than anyone else. It was a competitive drive that was birthed from a mother and father that always believed in me and poured their energy and support into me. They were there at the critical times in my youth when this young Underdog was beginning to develop. I will be forever grateful for my parents always being there and sacrificing for me when I was young. I can't put the impact of their presence into words. I'll suffice it to say that it did give me a competitive advantage though. Whether it was spotting them in a crowd of 200 or a crowd of 90,000, when I saw them the focus was intense. Their consistent support was evident whether it was from my mom being the cheerleading mom when I was young or my dad schooling me in the drive way shooting ball while talking trash to me. Oh, and for all of you that know me and how much trash I've talked when competing, it's entirely my dad's fault. Their support turned me into a driven, competitive person that just wanted to make his parents proud. Then it turned into a driven, competitive person that just wanted his team to win. I think that my success in athletics has never been about me. I have always been a team guy so I have always driven myself to prove people wrong because I guess that I viewed the doubters as doubting not just me but doubting my team. Whether it was doubting Team Covington (Mom & Dad) or whatever athletic team I was playing for. If you doubted me then you doubted us all and I wasn't having that. I wouldn't bet against me if I were you. I have taken that same approach into my corporate life as well. This book is a journey of the adversities and blessings that have touched my life over the years and how they have helped me to grow. My adversities will be different from your adversities. My blessings will be different from your blessings. My hope is that this book will be a steppingstone towards establishing belief in yourself and a belief that you can overcome anything that you set your mind on. I hope that it will make you want to reflect on your life and examine some of the things that you learned during some of your darkest hours. I hope that you will be willing to dig deep to find the positives in those tough times and just think about what blessing resulted from them. Sometimes it's painful to go back and revisit tough times, but if the past is holding you hostage from growing then you have to take that journey. You owe it to yourself to break the chains of your past so that you can create that future that you really want for yourself. Greatness is waiting for you. If anyone tells you that you can't be great or that you don't deserve your blessings, I want you to do three things:

1. Politely smile.
2. Whisper in their ear, "Kick rocks because I believe in ME!"
3. Look them in the eyes with a cold stare and tell them "I wouldn't bet against me if I were you, because... I AM UNDERDOG!"

# CHAPTER 1

## Heaven Needed an Angel

I REMEMBER GETTING the phone call from my dad telling me that I needed to make my way home because mom wasn't doing too well. I remember asking him if need to come home immediately and him telling me to wait until the next day. I was in DC visiting friends and he wanted me to take my time and have a full day to get home. I left DC, stopped in Charlottesville to grab some things and then made my way to North Carolina. As I turned onto my street, I saw all of these cars with out-of-state license plates. As I walked into a house full of relatives, a hush came over the room. I walked across the living room to greet my Aunt Sandy, my mom's sister. She hugged me and started crying. I told her everything was going to be alright. That mom was going to beat this thing. Just then my dad called me into my room and closed the door behind me. He told me that mom had passed away. I collapsed in his arms crying uncontrollably. It felt like someone had punched straight through my chest and pulled out my heart. She had taken her last breath on July 2, 1991. She was the most amazing woman I have ever met. I may be slightly biased but who cares. She was my best friend, my mother, my everything. She was gone at 47 years young, but she left footprints on my heart that took me a while to find and to follow. To talk only about the end of her life would diminish the incredible person she was so I will tell you about how she lived.

I never knew that one person could affect so much change on the people that she came in contact with. She was just a country girl from Axton, Virginia, who was always giving of her time and her money. Now be clear, we were not rich by any stretch, but she and my father worked hard to provide for the family. Neither of my parents had a college education but they were *educated*. Her parents were hard working farmers and I spent many summers in the house that she grew up in following my grandfathers every step. I reference the house and place that she grew up in because you have to know where this Angel was born and raised. The oldest daughter of Henry and Viola Hairston, she and her one sister, Sandy, and four brothers, Pee Wee, Robert, Donny and Tommy, lived in a 3-bedroom house with an attic and no in-home toilet. In those days folks had an outhouse, which was the only part I didn't like about those summers, but mom always insisted that I go and I was okay with it to be honest. There were lessons to be learned from those summers spent in the country and my mom knew that. A method to her madness, that as a child I just didn't understand. She wanted me to learn to appreciate whatever you have, be it a little or a lot. They didn't have a lot of money but man were they rich. She wanted me to see what it was like to work hard and to actually experience it, because it's hard to get where you want to go in life without working hard for it. Through those summer experiences I learned to never be afraid of hard work. She wanted me to learn the importance of family and what those bonds were really all about. I will never forget those Sunday mornings in the country and the breakfast spread that was laid out before us. It was a feast and everything was fresh from the farm and truly homemade. My grandmother was an amazing cook and she took care of that house. She made sure that she was in tune with everything that went on there. She was also a very giving person. If a neighbor or friend was in need she was there to lend a helping hand. She was a loving woman and she always made me feel loved and supported. Then there were the entertaining conversations on the porch after breakfast with my grandfather, who we called Pawpaw. He was a serious man but so dang funny at the same time. He had to be serious. He was the bread winner, a farmer helping to raise a black family in rural Axton, Virginia. I listened to him talk about the challenges and lack of resources he had to endure while raising his family. His loss of a son, Pee Wee, to pneumonia. His face, framed by thick eyebrows, always bore such a serious look, which I'm convinced was meant to discourage people from approaching him. It never discouraged me though because I worshipped him. I was drawn to his strength, his sense of humor, his work ethic and his commanding presence. He would get up before the sun came up. And right on his heels I could always be found, whether in the old pick-up truck or on the tractor. Whatever we did, rest assured, it was a full day of hard work. In later years, I came to realize that my mother gained so many of her qualities and virtues from her parents. Love of family, strength of purpose, work ethic, determination, honesty, integrity… I could go on and on. She was certainly part Pawpaw and part Grandma.

My mother was always a fighter and a survivor. She was never one to complain. We both almost died from pneumonia when I was born. She taught me to fight before I knew what it was to fight. She was my strength before I knew what it was to be strong. She was my blessing before I knew what it was to be blessed. I remember the car rides to my sporting events. I remember her being the cheerleading mom when I started playing football. She was always ever present and she may have missed one game in all of my years of playing sports. She taught me the importance of supporting your children in their endeavors. She worked her butt off to pay for drama classes, summer enrichment programs or whatever she felt would give me exposure to the many opportunities that were out there for me. The one caveat was that I had to make good grades. That was non-negotiable. She taught me that education would be the linchpin to whatever I wanted to do in the future. If I wanted to be an athlete, then she had my back. If I wanted to be an actor, then she had my back. She taught me to have confidence before I knew what it meant to be confident. Just knowing that she was there, gave me the confidence that I could do anything. I will never forget being able to find her and my dad amongst the tens of thousands of people at football games when I was in college. Once I saw them in the crowd, and that thousand-watt smile of hers flashed, rest assured my confidence was on 10 and my opponents would feel my fury that day.

That smile of hers changed people's lives. The people at our church called her "Smiley" because of the way that her smile affected people. She was very involved in the church so you know that meant that I had to be involved in the church. She was on the choir so I was on the junior usher board. But don't be fooled, she also had that look that said; "Boy if you don't sit your butt down and act right, I've got something for you." That's all it took for me. In fact, the other kids around me knew that look too and it made them "act right" as well. She had that effect on people. She would smile and turn their frowns into smiles. She always made people feel better. People borrowed money from her knowing they had no intention of ever paying her back. She gave of her time without expecting anything in return. I remember getting on her case about that and just telling her that those people were just taking advantage of her. She would just smile and say that it was okay and not to worry about it. She taught me the importance of giving before I understood that we make a life by what we give. She dedicated her life to service and gave me the example of what that meant before I could even think about grasping the concept. She wasn't just my angel and my blessing; she was an angel and a blessing for countless others.

She called my one day during my second year in college. The call started out in our typical fashion. Mom asked what I was doing and I said that I had just returned to my room to watch my recorded soap operas before heading to workout. (For the record, this was our conversation almost daily. I would call her and ask what she was doing, and she would say that she was working and then she would ask me the same question. We were two peas in a pod.) She said she had something to tell me. I said, "Shoot." The next words that followed were "I have been diagnosed with breast cancer." It felt like my world ended in that moment. The gravity of the word cancer caved in my world like 100 elephants crushing me one by one. I laid on my bed, wanting to know everything, as tears streamed down my face. All I knew was that people got cancer and then they died. How was a nineteen-year-old, whose mother was the center of his world supposed to handle something like that? Let's just say I didn't respond too well. The kid who once was so full of confidence and charisma became a zombie, a shell of the vibrant person people had looked to for leadership. I shut out most of my friends and my coaches and internalized it all. My grades went south and my performance during spring football was awful, prompting my coaches to ask me what the hell was wrong with me. Academically, I was studying but I was distracted. I could see the words on the page but they meant nothing. I just couldn't focus. Athletically, football just wasn't important to me in that moment, and so I was literally going through the motions. My reason for making good grades and playing sports was over three hours away battling against, what I felt, was an unbeatable opponent. While she was telling me to be strong, all I wanted to do was hug her. The chemotherapy and radiation treatments were brutal and I could see its effects on my mom when I got to see her. You have to remember, I'm talking about cancer of the 1980's when they didn't have the kind of information and treatments they have today. The struggle for my mom was real, but the one thing it couldn't dull was her million-watt smile. We continued to talk almost daily, all the while she kept telling me she was going to be fine. My mother never lied to me, so I believed her. I could see the weight loss and the hair loss. It frightened me, but if she was scared she didn't show it. She stayed strong and kept telling me to stay focused. But how could I when my mother, my everything, was going through hell?

After chemotherapy and radiation treatments, she returned to her oncologists and they told her there were no traces of the cancer, and that it had gone into remission. I was overcome with a sense of relief and once again all was right with the world. My focus returned and my grades immediately improved, as did my play on the field. I finally opened up about what I had been going through and my coaches wanted to know why I hadn't said anything. All I could say was that it was a personal matter and I decided to deal with it on my own. After the fact, I realized I could have handled it better. Mom always preached family first and my coaches and team really were an extension of my family. My coaches were right when they told me we are all family and I shouldn't have had chosen to shoulder losing my mom alone. In hindsight, I understand that maybe I was being selfish or maybe I was just scared and my defense mechanism defaulted to shut down and internalize. Whatever the case may have been, my mom was better and she never stopped smiling during her battle. There were so many times her smile made everything better for me and to know she had the love of so many family and friends made it better for her. There is something to be said for knowing that you're loved and needed. I think my mom always knew she was loved and needed but there is nothing like being told through words and actions. Her smile has been etched into so many of my memories. I remember walking across the Lawn at the University of Virginia on graduation day. I was dressed in my cap and gown with purple and gold shoe laced combat boots on my way to hear the commencement address and to receive my diploma at a ceremony at one of the gardens. The professor said, "Anthony L. Covington," and a friend hollered out, "Just Do it!" I replied, "I just did it" and I looked at my mother and that smile was beaming enough to light up a deep, dark forest that had never been exposed to light. What made that day great was remembering all of the sacrifices my parents had made to get me— the first in my family to receive a college degree—to that place, at that moment. My mother, my everything, had endured much in her battle with cancer and she gave me life, with her love and her smile.

I had one more season of college eligibility remaining and mom and dad were in the crowd watching me have one hell of a season. The season ended with a game in New Orleans, at the Sugar Bowl. Then I played in a senior all-star game in Tokyo, the Japan Bowl. That was followed by an exemplary showing at the NFL Combine. Things were trending in the right direction until we found out that the cancer had returned after three years. I watched my mom start to deteriorate. She said she was fine and told me to continue to stay focused, so that's what I did. I remember the day I got the phone call that the Tampa Bay Buccaneers had selected me in the fourth round of the NFL draft. I ran upstairs and told her she would never have to work again, and her smile was just amazing. She just sat there in the bed smiling. I hugged her and then she told me how proud she was of me. I have never forgotten that moment and I never will. I was right about one thing; she would never have to work again because she was gone three months later. She was forty-seven years young. How in the hell does that happen? How does this happen to an angel? I knew my mom hadn't been looking well, but she would tell me that she was doing okay and that she was going to beat this thing. When the cancer came back, it returned with a vengeance. It had metastasized and spread throughout her body. There was nothing more the doctors could do. She was terminal, and I appeared to be the only one that didn't know. I could have been upset at my family for not telling me that she was dying, and maybe somewhere in my deep subconscious I was a little upset, but I never let them see it. In hindsight, I don't fault them for keeping me in the dark because I hadn't handled her initial cancer diagnosis very well at nineteen and so they were concerned about how I would handle it at twenty-two. My dad and sister were there daily and my Aunt Linda was there more often than not. They had watched how much pain she had gone through and how much she had suffered. My Aunt Linda was there at the end reading Psalm 23 to mom. She told me that in those last minutes mom said, "GO!" Initially Aunt Linda thought mom was telling her to go, but as mom took what would be her last breath and Linda asked the nurse if she was gone, she understood that "GO" meant something different. Mom was telling her that she was going. They had been best friends before I was ever born and I always viewed Aunt Linda as a second mom. She officially became my aunt when she married mom's brother Donny. She called mom, Prince, her nickname. The two had been inseparable in life. She looked up as if witnessing mom's spirit leaving and said she would see her again. I know that it was difficult for her to say goodbye, but at least she got to say goodbye. One thing that has always bothered me and still haunts me today is that I never got to say goodbye. Even as I write this, I feel a tug at the scar on my heart and my eyes begin to water. I've tried to make sense out of it for over two decades now and that pain just abates but never truly goes away. And although I still feel cheated that I didn't get to say goodbye, I know that mom wanted it that way.  My sister, Melanie, was away on a field trip in Washington, DC and I too was also in DC hanging with friends.  I remember asking mom if she wanted me to stay home but she told me to go hang with my friends and that she was okay.  She knew the end was near and didn't want to put either of us through those last moments.  My sister had been with her in North Carolina every day watching our mom suffer, and I never really knew the lasting effect that it had on her until we were much older.  I appreciate my mom for wanting us not to be there at the end, but I needed those last moments to say goodbye.  I needed to tell my best friend, my angel, my everything that I would miss her and how much she had meant to me.  I needed to say goodbye and tell her that I would always love her.  I don't think that my heart will ever stop crying because I didn't get the chance to do that.  Her intentions were good and I guess there was no perfect way to handle it, but it caused anger and I could only direct my anger at God because I felt like He made a mistake.  A woman who missed one game in all of my years of playing sports would never get to see her son play on one of the biggest stages, the National Football League.  In a world with so many criminals and bad people, how could He take her?  How could He take my Angel?  Didn't He know I needed her?  We laid my mother to rest and people came from everywhere.  There were cars lined up for miles and the church was standing room only.  I remember the last time I looked at her face in the casket.  I placed my college jersey in the casket with her because I felt she would have it no other way.  So many people were crying that day, both at the church and at the grave site.  They lowered her into the ground and I was virtually in a daze.  Thank God, I had so many of my childhood and college friends along with family there with me.  I needed them those first couple of days after her funeral, because they were a struggle.  She had impacted so many people in her short lifetime.  She was a testament to the saying *"it's not how many days that you get, but it's what you do with the days that you get."*

I left North Carolina the following week and moved to Tampa, Florida, where I knew no one, to try and earn a spot on an NFL roster. It was one of the loneliest times of my life. I'm so thankful for a little-known rookie at the time, Marty Carter, and a veteran player, Ricky Reynolds. They helped tremendously with my transition into the NFL. In fact, Ricky would continue to play a critical role in my life both during and after my NFL career. I have to admit I was lost for a minute. Mom had always turned to prayer in good and bad times. I remembered that lesson and I wanted to pray but just couldn't. Well, I wouldn't pray. I would attend the pre-game chapel services before games, but it was just my body sitting there. I was still too angry at God to open up and believe again. It was as if the meaning behind mom taking me to church all those times had disappeared. I no longer trusted Him. Hell, maybe I didn't trust myself anymore. But there I was, trying to make an NFL roster and relying on one thing I was very good at and that was playing football. It had always been my first love and it became my sanctuary that allowed me to push all of the pain, frustration, anger, love and loss deep inside of me. It helped to mask everything that I was going through. I had always been thankful for the God given abilities that were bestowed upon me, but this anger thing clouded how I now felt about it. But, I made the 53-man roster and had an outstanding rookie season. I was named a starter for the Tampa Bay Buccaneers at strong safety at 188 pounds. My friend and fellow rookie, Marty Carter, was the starter at free safety and Ricky Reynolds was the starting corner and always had the assignment of guarding the opponent's best wide receiver. Now Ricky was an outstanding player and lead by example. He wasn't very vocal and he played at an extremely high level. I was labeled as "his" rookie and he took me under his wing and showed me how to be a professional. I, on the other hand, was very vocal and played with a lot of enthusiasm. Translation: I talked a lot of trash, but backed it up with my play. I was the guy who would listen to his rap music before the game and then hit the field amped up out of my mind. I could be found jumping in my teammates faces, high fiving and head-butting them. Ricky would often say that I would get him too hyped. I remember him telling me that the team hadn't had anybody like me around there in a long time. That was refreshing to me because I played the game because I loved the game and I loved the physicality of the sport. I viewed it as a gladiator sport. The greatest team sport on the planet. I loved to compete and my intensity was clearly apparent. I called the defense and some of the veteran players actually looked to me for leadership. I thought that was odd initially, considering the amount of money that those guys were making, but on the field money didn't matter and everyone wasn't built to lead. People have always gravitated toward me for my leadership, so I got over it and realized that this was just one of those times and I was okay with that.

As a team, we struggled mightily though. I wasn't used to losing the way we lost. I had helped to turn my collegiate team into a winning program so I was used to winning. The losing started to get to me as I was leaving the field after a loss at Miami where I had about fifteen tackles. As I left the field, I felt a hand on my shoulder pad and an encouraging voice tell me to keep working hard because I was going to be one hell of a player. Those encouraging words came from Dan Marino. Man, I felt really blessed in that moment because he didn't have to do that. I told him that I really appreciated his words and jogged to the locker room with a little pep in my step. In the locker room, Ricky came over to me and told me to not get caught up in the losing and to work on one aspect of my game every single day. I did just that and my play continued to go to new levels. I never forgot those words and have shared them with many an athlete that I have coached or mentored. Those words guided me to earn All-Rookie honors leading all rookie safeties in tackles and interceptions. My mother would have been proud. What she would not have been proud of however was what my life had become outside of the playing field. Because I was still angry at God, I took on this belief; "Tony" was the reason that I had success. I wasn't praying nor was I attending church. I partied and drank and was just lost. I told myself that I didn't need Him after all and that I had put in all the work, so why not enjoy the fruits of "my" labor, earned from "my" abilities. I was an idiot of epic proportions but hey, as I said earlier, I was lost and didn't even know it.

The offseason after a successful rookie campaign, the team wanted to sign me to a long-term contract but they wanted to move me to free safety from strong safety. They told my agent that if he proves that he can handle the transition then the Monday after the first regular season game, then we would get the deal done. I would let the team and the agent handle that part of things, because I wanted to get back to doing what I do and the Phoenix Cardinals, as they were called in 1992, were on the schedule as our home opener. I woke up the morning of the game out of sorts. I had a dream about my mother and she kept walking away from me. She would walk through a door and then I would try to follow her and I could never catch her. I screamed in her direction, why are you doing this? It was if she was playing some kind of game. I woke up and went into the bathroom as not to disturb my roommate. I got myself together and then did my normal pre-game ritual. I had a heightened sense of anger at the start of this game. Be clear, I played with anger and fury all of the time but this was different. I got an early penalty for unnecessary roughness and my anger would just not abate. Right before the half, the Cardinals had the ball inside of two minutes to go and I recognized the formation and got a jump on the play. I eluded the blocker and went to make the tackle and my knee just buckled. I was down and it wasn't good. They brought the cart on the field to get me and as I left the field, I was barking to my teammates to kick their asses and the crowd was going crazy. I got into the locker room and told them to get me a knee sleeve so I could be ready for the second half. The trainers told me to hit the showers and report to the orthopedic surgeon's office the next morning. They couldn't determine much from the MRI but set an appointment for surgery two days later. Before they administered the anesthesia, the surgeon told me that he was going to do arthroscopic surgery with a laser and that if it was just some cartilage damage then I would be out for four weeks. However, if he got in there I found something significant then my season would be over. He said if you wake up in recovery with an ace bandage on the knee then you know its short-term but if there is a brace up to your hip then there was more damage and we would be looking at a more long-term situation. As he applied the anesthesia, my last words were, "take care of me, Doc." They woke me up in recovery and I reached for my leg. I felt the brace all the way up to my hip and started screaming and cussing and swinging at anyone that was in arm's length. I absolutely lost it and let's just say, that they made sure that I went back to sleep. Gone was the season, the long-term contract and I was staring at a long rehabilitation. This was my first Charlie Sheen (Bud Foster) moment in the movie Wall Street, when Lou said to Bud, "A man looks into the abyss and see's nothing looking back at him...that's when he finds his character and that's what keeps him from going into the abyss!" The crazy thing about the injury was that no one was near me. The coaches said it was the darnedest thing because I was in open field and I just went down. When I went through rehab, the coaches' words kept echoing in my head. I had reconstructive knee surgery on Sept. 8th of that year and I was home in North Carolina for Thanksgiving standing at the top of a hill that we called "The Bank" at my high school. "The Bank" was massive and we used it for training in high school and we always knew that no team worked as hard as we did or put their trust in "The Bank" like we did. So, there I was standing at the top of "The Bank" in the rain, in thirty-two-degree weather... ALONE. I went to work. What drove me were the words of the doctor telling me that I might not play again. He didn't know that he was talking to the eternal Underdog and that people had told me that I wouldn't/couldn't do things all of my life. Never count out the Underdog and I have proven a lot of people wrong over my lifetime. I left the school that day with a sense of confidence because I knew that I was on track for a return. I went back to Tampa but there was something changing about me. I began to reflect more deeply on a lot of things in my life that had happened to me. I was evolving. When I went back home to spend my Christmas holidays with my family, I was different. On New Year's Eve, I was in the bedroom where I spent most of my high school years and I bowed to my knees for the first time in a long time. What had changed about me was that it had become abundantly clear that I could not live a life without God in it. I asked Him to forgive me and told Him that I couldn't live without Him. I grew into understanding that He never makes mistakes and that He needed to take my Angel because she was HIS Angel before she was ever mine. He needed her because He had work for her to do in Heaven and that her assignments on Earth had reached their conclusion. He placed on my heart that He was the one that gifted me all of my abilities and that I was supposed to lean on Him and give Him all the praise. He let me know that I am special because I am His child and not because of anything that I had accomplished. He instructed me that He took the game away from me, temporarily, because He needed me to come back to Him. Your mother was your blessing and now she is being a blessing to others. I know that you were hurt and I am sorry for that, but she is with me and you will have to be all right with that. I forgave you before you even asked me too. Now put your hand in mine and leave the weight that you have been carrying at my feet. I rose from my knees with the biggest smile on my face and it felt like the weight of the world had been lifted from my shoulders. I had found my way back to Him and I would need Him because the journey was just beginning. My mother carried so many of us on her earthly angel wings and in hindsight; that must have been a heavy load. But she never wavered and she never stopped smiling.

ADVERSITY: Losing my best friend, my mother, my everything.
BLESSING: Obtaining a more spiritual understanding and relationship with God.

# CHAPTER 2

## Sometimes the Game Quits You

THERE IS ONE thing definitive about sports, it has an end date and most of the time you do not get to choose that date. After making it back from knee surgery and playing four years for Tampa, I was a free agent. I had finally bought my first home because my future was bright and I was going to be working for the next contract to pay it off over the next few seasons. Free agents travel to teams that are interested in them and have individual workouts and interviews with the coaches. I visited the Miami Dolphins, the Jacksonville Jaguars, the New York Jets and the Pittsburgh Steelers. Miami would have been awesome, but after visiting Pittsburgh I found where I wanted to be. I had a tremendous workout with them and my conversations with the defensive backs coach in talking schemes went very well. Coach Cowher popped his head into that meeting and flat out asked if I could help the Pittsburgh Steelers and the coach said, "Absolutely." Coach Cowher and I watched my field workout and then he showed me the workouts of some other potential players for whom the Steelers had an interest. Maybe I'm a little biased, but they couldn't touch my workout. The thing that I liked about Coach Cowher was that he was transparent. He told me that I would play about fifty-five percent the coming season and that they would probably lose one of their starters to free agency the following season, so they didn't want to have any drop off. I said that made perfect sense to me and that I wanted to be there so let's get the deal done.

Enter the business side of professional sports. The Steelers proposed a two-year deal with an option for a third year. My agent countered with a straight two-year deal, but they wouldn't budge. Suddenly, I found myself on the way to Seattle for a meeting with the Seahawks. They told me everything that my agent and I wanted to hear, most importantly a two-year contract. In hindsight, I signed a career killing two-year contract with the Seattle Seahawks. Hindsight is such an evil word. A former teammate from Tampa, who was then with Steelers told me that they just knew they had me and were pissed that I didn't sign with them. They wondered why in the world I would go to Seattle when the Steelers were contending for Super Bowl Championships on a consistent basis. How could I have known that Rod Woodson would go down with a season-ending knee injury and safety, Carnell Lake, would move to cornerback opening up a spot to start at safety for yours truly? And they did represent the American Football Conference in the Super Bowl that season. DAMN! DAMN! DAMN! Scratch that. Hindsight is worse than evil. It is that knife in your back that is out of your reach so you just slowly bleed out until you die. Why didn't I sign with the Steelers again? Well, the two-year contract with an option for a third year didn't make financial sense at the time. Let me break it down. Remember that Coach Cowher said that I would play fifty-five percent that first year and that they felt that they would lose one of their safeties to free agency in year two? Well, I would have been making back-up money the first season, since rightfully I would've been a backup. But, in year two as a starter I would've been making back-up money with an option year that they controlled, and I could have still been making the same back-up money. It was a bad financial contract for me, but if I had known what I was walking into in Seattle I would have taken that bad financial contract in Pittsburgh. DAMN! DAMN! DAMN! AGAIN! A career college coach in his first year in the NFL and a lack of transparency from the start with my position coach and the Seattle experience was doomed before it started. I spent time between playing special teams and being inactive. The starting two safeties were high paid guys and the three of us that were back-ups had enough talent to be playing for other teams. There just wasn't enough airtime for everyone. I asked myself, "What in the hell do you do when you are on the bench?" I had never experienced that in my life other than being redshirted my first year in college. Did I handle this well? I surely did not. Did I tell the head coach that I didn't feel like a part of the team? Yes, I surely did. Should I have kept my thoughts to myself? I probably should have, but he called me in his office to talk and the opportunity to speak truth was there so I took it. I couldn't wait for that season to be over and get back to Tampa to train and work on my business ventures.

Our last game of the season was at Kansas City and I was inactive, again. When the game was over I flew straight to Tampa from Kansas City. I needed to regroup and get myself together. I went home and hired a trainer and worked out the entire offseason with some of my former Buccaneer teammates that were with other teams now as well. Nothing like working out with guys that have bled with you on the field of battle and possess a dedication that mirrors yours. Meanwhile, Seattle was in the process of trying to move to Los Angeles only to be forced to move back to Seattle by the Commissioner of the NFL. They wanted as many guys to come back and train with the team as possible, but it wasn't mandatory. I decided to stay in Tampa and showed up to Seattle for training camp in the best shape of my career. It was a contract year and I was determined to get on the field to show what I could do. My teammates were blown away by how impressive I looked after training so hard in Tampa, and so were the coaches. The head coach told me that I was obviously not one that they had to worry about coming into camp out of shape, and the defensive coordinator said that he had big plans for me. I had a good camp despite a nagging groin injury that I got on punt return late in the fourth quarter of the first preseason game. I missed the second preseason game because of the injury, and my defensive coordinator thought it best I rehab and rest my groin because he didn't want that injury to linger into the season. I was rehabbing three times a day trying to be ready for the third preseason game in Indianapolis. I had a good game and was getting my mind ready for the regular season. Then I get the call the next day that coach wanted to see me and to bring my playbook. Coach said they were going to take a chance on some younger guys, but that there was a lot of interest out there in me. I shook his hand and thanked him for the opportunity. They told my agent, however, that they wanted to take a chance on some younger guys because they wouldn't have to pay them what they would have to pay me. I got one call during the season and it was between another safety and me. The other guy had played for the coach with another team so he got the nod over me. This is where your agent is supposed to earn his money and really work his ass off for his client. Needless to say, that didn't happen. I kept training trying to keep the dream alive. "It can't be over yet," I thought, "I'm only twenty-eight years old."

I was able to get myself a workout for the San Francisco 49ers because their special teams coach was the former special teams coach in Tampa. I had a great workout and afterwards the defensive backs coach said that I looked great and that he couldn't tell that I had missed a season at all. He asked what happened in Seattle. I told him that they told me they wanted to take a chance on some younger guys. The coach said that I had some more years left in me and that they needed a veteran safety that could play both positions and I fit the bill. The one caveat was that they were trying to upgrade their cornerback situation and were targeting

Rod Woodson. If they signed him they would not have enough money available to offer me a contract. I thanked him and told him that was fair and that I hoped to hear from him soon. They signed Rod Woodson and I never played professional football again.

I went home and kept training still trying to hold on to the dream. I think that I wanted to go out on my own terms and to not have the NFL divorce me. I had one more shot to make it back, but it would be through the World League. I was a first-round draft pick by the Barcelona Dragons. Training camp was to be held in Atlanta, but I was skeptical. I had strained something in my lower back a little while training and having had back surgery three years previously, I kept thinking that if I get hurt in the World League that I'd never make it back to the NFL. I also thought to myself that I shouldn't have to prove I can still play by doing it in the World League in Spain, of all places. I don't have many regrets in my life, but not throwing caution to the wind and giving the World League a shot is one of them. When I decided not to go to their training camp, at the time it really seemed to make sense. I was still hopeful that I would get that call from the NFL and I guess I didn't really view the World League as a steppingstone. I talked to an agent that I was interested in hiring and he shared some information that hit me like a ton of bricks. He told me that I had been blackballed and labeled a prima donna. I was devastated. A couple of months after that I was golfing at a celebrity event with a former Miami Hurricane football player and he told me what really happened in Seattle. He told me that I had pissed them off because I hadn't gone out to Seattle to train in the offseason. The coaching world is a fraternity, and if a bad word gets put out there about a player it is the kiss of death. After gaining insight from the agent as well as my friend, the picture began to take focus. None of it made sense to me, but maybe it wasn't supposed to make sense. In fact, it was all part of

God's greater plan for my life. Maybe He was saving me from a devastating injury. It's all speculation, but I have learned never to question the motives of the Master and to trust His decisions. He was closing a door because another one would eventually be opening. It didn't feel like it at the time, but He was working all things out for the good. But there would be plenty of struggles waiting for me on the horizon.

ADVERSITY: Having my job and the game that I loved taken away from me, seemingly prematurely.
BLESSING: Getting paid for playing a game that I love, which enabled me to help family and friends along the way.

# CHAPTER 3

## The Struggle Was Real

MY FOOTBALL CAREER was over, but I'm a graduate of the University of Virginia so I will be just fine, or so I thought. I had a major business venture that I was shopping around with my partners and we had meetings with all types of potential investors. We visited Magic Johnson in Los Angeles, Mike Tyson's people and all types of venture capitalists. I even invested some of my own money, but we could never secure the major investor that we needed. It was apparent that the business venture wasn't going to happen as quickly as we had hoped. It was such a great concept and all of the numbers made sense. It was a line of family indoor entertainment centers. Now remember, this was in the early to mid '90's and at that time there wasn't much competition in the space. We envisioned a place for families to visit with something for every age group to do. It was akin to going to an amusement park, combined with a carnival, with a splash of Chuck-e-Cheese, all indoors. It would feature affordable food and have an affordable admission price. The business plan was strong and the returns were projected to be lucrative but ultimately, we were a startup, and while a number of investors really loved the concept they wanted to see one be successful first before they would be willing to come on board. Unfortunately, we could not make that happen, financially, so the entire concept was shelved. It was the moment I feared because now the real world, with real bills, was starring me right in the face.

What is sobering about playing for the NFL is that the player's salaries are not guaranteed. A contract is really not worth the paper it's written on because it can be cancelled by the team at any time. In a perfect world, a player makes financial decisions based on the trajectory of his career. He puts away a portion of his salary for a rainy day while looking to build on his career. That sounds like a great plan, but then something happens on the way toward that long career. It gets cancelled before he thought it would and even though the player thought he was making smart decisions, ultimately, they were not smart enough. Big bills continue to come in and the big checks are no longer there to cover them. These are what I refer to as rainy days. I had put money away in case these days came. I finally invested in a home after my fourth year in the NFL and bought furniture for it. I bought myself a nice car to go along with my SUV and a couple of jet skis. Life was pretty good and I felt like I deserved some nice things. After all, I worked my ass off and put myself to the hazard every single week during the season. I worked my tail off in the offseason so that I could put the best product on the field. It all came crashing down with the words, "We're letting you go and there is a lot of interest out there in you!" Years later, people would say, "But you played in the NFL, you've got money or didn't you save your money?" If I would've known that after finally purchasing a home and a few toys for myself, my career would be over a year and half later, I would have never purchased any of it. The NFL is corporate big business at its finest. Here is an example for you. Picture a top executive that has worked his behind off for years to help build a company and then unceremoniously receives a pink slip for a younger, more inexpensive model with the hopes that they can replicate some of his productivity. The company severs ties with that executive and business goes on. They may sacrifice productivity in the short-term but they save in compensation, and it really boils down to dollars and cents. Is it fair? HELL NO! Unfortunately, it is business though. The timing couldn't have been worse. I made those investments because at 28 years old, my future was bright and was trending upward. The NFL didn't get that message, so they quit me. We broke up and they filed divorce papers. The creditors didn't get the memo that the NFL had divorced me and those bills kept coming. No one told the creditors that when the NFL divorces you that your income is shut down immediately. I had to use that rainy-day money, but after a while it was not enough. I had only put aside money for rain and it was storming in epic proportions. In the midst of this I started studying real estate and started studying the insurance industry. Nothing ever materialized from it.

I had a degree from the University of Virginia, but no work experience. As a result, the transition from NFL football player to the real world of finding a job was a difficult one, to say the least. I eventually got a sales job selling water treatment equipment. It was 100% commission and it was tough, but I got really good at it because I had no choice. I will give them credit for teaching some really unique sales techniques because they worked. I became one of the top salesmen in the area and received top sales awards. I would visit a potential customer's home to sell them a piece of equipment that was roughly $5,000 and I had three hours to show them what this investment would save them overall. I only had that night to close the deal or at least that's what I was told. I would find out that if the sale was not closed that night the company would call the potential customer back and sell it to them at a lower price the next day, and of course I got no credit for that. Something else that was crazy about the company was that my commission was based on the credit score of the prospects. In other words, if a prospect had

"A" credit then I could earn close to $1,000 off the sale, but if their credit was a little sketchy then I could earn only $39. The presentation was no different because I wouldn't know about credit scores going into the presentation. So, there I was, out busting my hump and getting screwed over a couple of different ways. It seems that every legal thing that I tried seemed to be coming up short.

During this brief period, I was exploring options of how to make some additional money. I got into the night club business with some shady characters, which resulted in people propositioning me to get into the drug business. How in the hell did I allow these unsavory people to infiltrate my circle? Man, you truly have to be careful of the company you keep. When times are tough, your character has to keep you out of the abyss. It didn't stop there, as I had a friend who was in the male companionship business, approach me about an opportunity. I would consider her a good friend and someone that I trusted. She said her and a couple of her friends would take care of all my bills if I would... How can I say this? "Manage them." She told me the three of them had a particular set of skills that brought in roughly $30,000 per month in cash, combined. It was damn near an offer I couldn't refuse. I said to myself, "Self?" Self answered, "Huh?" "How in the hell did we get here?" This is referred to as the proverbial crossroads on the highway of life. Ultimately, I said no to it all. I could see my mother staring at me from the choir stand. I couldn't go down that road because I hadn't been raised that way. I refused to disappoint her that way, even in death. Oh, remember the unsavory guys from the nightclub business, my brief encounter with them came back to haunt me as well. One day I get a knock at the door from two FBI agents. They attempted to coerce me into setting up a guy from the nightclub that I had been involved in, who turned out to be a big-time drug dealer. I had known the guy for a while and considered him a friend. I told them that I was no longer associated with the nightclub. They told me that they had confiscated my car at his home and I told them that he was attempting to sell it for me and that he had a buyer. They threatened me with all sorts of things but I refused to help them, because I didn't know that he was a big-time drug dealer. They then tried to get me to wear a wire and set up the guy that was going to buy my car, who I didn't even know. It was an absolute mess. I escorted them to the front door as they threatened to come back and make my life hell. I told them that they had my address and that I would be right there. Truth be told, I was absolutely terrified but never heard from them again. I did find out many years later that one of the agents was corrupt and was probably trying to shake me down. I heard he eventually was found out and got what was coming to him. The Feds kept my car and turned it over to Mercedes Benz, who had been looking for it since I was behind on the payments anyway. The Benz was gone, the SUV had been turned in, and of my two Jet Ski's, one had been stolen and the other had been returned. I was down to a motorcycle as my only means of transportation, while fighting off foreclosure on the house. I was a beaten man and just felt like I could bear no more.

It is during these times that God inserts angels in your life to make their presence felt and the angel that he sent was Ricky Reynolds. Ricky, my former teammate and good friend, saved my life. I just called him one day and he came over and we talked about everything. He told me that my heart was in the right place and I was a good man, but my focus was off. He told me that I was making all of the goals that I was seeking into idols. He said that I wasn't doing it for God but for self. He asked me if I had ever once consulted God about my plans or His plans for me. He told me until

I put God first in all things; I would be successful at nothing. "He brought you to this place for a reason," he said. "He demands that we rely on Him and trust in the plan that He has for our lives, even if we can't see the plan. So, trust in Him because He will never leave us nor forsake us." He told me that I was at the bottom and that there was nowhere to go but up. "Why not let God lead you?" he asked. He began to share the Word of God with me in a way that I had not experienced before, or moreover, been open to receiving before. I began to see myself in the pages of the Bible, specifically in Paul. He was one of the worst sinners and God forgave him. He became a changed man on the road to Damascus and began to live his life for God. As we were going through the Bible, a verse from Isaiah 30:21 stood out to me and has stayed with me ever since, as I feel it describes me in my walk with Christ. It states, "If you should leave the path and go astray, you will hear a voice say, NO, this is the way, walk here." This verse still carries the same importance for me all of these years later because it describes me to a tee. The Lord and I can be just walking hand in hand and everything is great and I suddenly hear the world calling me. Man, they are having so much fun in the world right now, Lord I'll be right back. Sure enough, 10 out of 10 times I have found myself stuck in the sticker briar bush reaching for the Lord who never took another step without me. He helps me out of the thorny rose bush, helps remove the thorns out of my behind, smiles and takes my hand in His. He forgives me before I can ask for forgiveness because I am His. I gained the understanding that because I have a relationship with Him, my burdens are not mine to bear alone and that even in times of trial and tribulation He is there. He is the one constant when all others abandon us and He is all we need. I have learned that I can overcome anything with Him at my side and that I can do nothing without Him.  I am a work in progress but my God is a patient God. I thank Him for loving me in spite of myself.

ADVERSITY: Losing a lot of material things I had worked hard to obtain.
BLESSING: Ricky Reynolds, my earthly angel, finding me on my own personal road to Damascus and saving me.

# CHAPTER 4

## Love, Marriage and Divorce

I HAVE TO give my ex-wife, Leslie, a shout-out because I have known her for over 24 years and she is one of the strongest women I have ever known. I consider her one of my best friends and I thank God for her. We first met back in 1992. She had come to Tampa with her friend, Donna, who I knew and they were headed on a cruise. I got a call from my friend, Diane, saying she and Donna were going to swing by and that she had another friend from Philly who she wanted me to meet. I was in the process of moving to a new place so I was just at home packing. I happened to have a friend in town visiting me. It was a friend who I had been introduced to by a teammate. This chick had a game plan and I saw right through it. I was just waiting for the weekend to be over so I could drop her off at the airport. The doorbell rings and I tell them to come in because I was knee deep in boxes and bubble wrap. Diane, Donna and then Leslie walk into the house. When I saw Leslie, my jaw hit the floor. Hazel eyes? Check. Nice figure? Check. Long hair? Check. Cool swagger about her? Check. She was confident, independent and she knew she was bad. She had all the pre-requisites: looks, brains and gainful employment. On a side note, I realized as I got older that the whole "pre-requisite" thing is total BS. Go with who you like/love and let the chips fall where they may. My mom always told me to make sure a young lady brought something of value to the table. What she meant was that there had to be substance there as well, and not to just fall for a pretty face. I wanted to know more about her because the first impression had me sold. So, they went on their cruise and I picked them up on their return trip and persuaded them to stay a couple of extra days in Tampa. We got to talk and I liked what I heard. Man, this chick had flavor.

We stayed in contact and she returned to Tampa for a visit. I then went to Philly for a wedding and she accompanied me. We dated off and on for eight years or so, with moves to Seattle, Philly and finally Tampa before I asked her to marry me. We got married in Maui, Hawaii and had our reception in Virginia at her father's home, where a lot of friends and family came to celebrate our nuptials. She was with me during a lot of those years of struggle as a professional football player and during the transitional years that followed. We were dating long distance a majority of the eight years, so she didn't realize the full extent of things because I chose not to share that with her. When I asked her to marry me I was on the tail end of my major financial struggle. The bank was looking to foreclose on my home and I found several loopholes to keep them at bay, giving myself time to come up with a solution. I eventually found a way but before I did, a sheriff showed up at the door when I wasn't home one day and revealed the potential foreclosure information. I had worked things out and hoped that I could keep this one close to the vest because I didn't want to stress her out, as we were expecting our first child. She was a worrier and I didn't want her to feel the pressure that I knew I could handle. In my mind, that thought process made perfect sense or maybe it's just a guy thing. I didn't realize until years later how that decision impacted her. We progressed and then welcomed our first child into the world. The first time I held Kennedy Logan in my arms my heart melted. I never knew that I could love like that. I held her so that her mother could see her for the first time and I couldn't stop smiling. I will never forget that day.

We seemed to survive that time period, and eventually sold the house on our terms. We found some property just south of Tampa and built another home. Things seemed to be looking up as we both had decent jobs, a roof over our heads, reliable transportation, and a beautiful child with another on the way. During this time, I became a marathon/half marathon runner as a byproduct of my job, which was a development officer for a marathon training program that focused on raising money for stroke research and education. Plus, running created a place of peace for me. We both were working hard as we welcomed our second child, Carter Monroe, into the world. That same type of emotion enveloped me just as it had when I first held Kennedy. We anxiously waited for her to be cleared to come home, as she had jaundice and had to stay in the hospital a couple of extra days. Those two are the best things that have ever happened to me. I can't even describe the feelings and sense of responsibility that I felt knowing that I was now the protector of two daughters. I was so thankful and just knew that I was blessed beyond measure. However, despite these two incredible blessings, everything was not right with the marriage. We had kind of lost our way. On the surface, appeared a functioning family, but behind closed doors we were merely roommates. We lost the intimacy and communication that makes for a healthy and vibrant relationship. We sought guidance from our Pastor as well as individual counselors and a couple's counselor. We both found out a lot about ourselves in the individual counseling sessions, but by the time we went to couples counseling it was already close to the end. I remember walking into the counseling session and her sitting at one end of the couch and me at the other. The counselor asked why we were sitting apart and neither of us even realized that we were. But at home, when we actually did sleep in the same bed, we slept that way too and unconsciously we were living that way—separated. One day, Kennedy asked me why mommy and I didn't sleep in the same bed or hug each other, because she was so used to me showering her and her sister with so much affection. It was a punch in the gut because I realized we were giving our daughters a poor example of a healthy and loving relationship. I had also changed in that the diehard romantic, affectionate and loving person I believed myself to be, no longer existed. I felt taken for granted and not appreciated. I lost a majority of myself and the person that I had always been. I was missing what I needed so I put my focus into our kids, my job and the team I was coaching. I stopped communicating and just kept my head down and grinded through. People can exist like that forever and be totally content, but I couldn't do it once I realized the example that I was setting. I remember walking into my office one day where we had a huge collage of pictures of staff, volunteers and marathon participants from our different events around the country. There was a little picture of me in the bunch with this smile on my face that just reached out to me. It was a smile that was eerily similar to my mother's smile. I asked myself, "What happened to that guy?" I realized I was just existing and trying to be there for my kids and it wasn't enough for any of us. We all deserved better.

Divorce entered the conversation between us during a trip to Pennsylvania for the Christmas holiday. It was an uncomfortable conversation, but one that we needed to have. I saw things one way and she saw them another way. There was some silence and there was some arguing. We left Pennsylvania with no resolution from that conversation, but the very real possibility of divorce was now on the table. During the flight back to Florida, Leslie started to feel a little faint and handed Carter to me. She suddenly slumped over in her seat and passed out. When we landed, the EMTs rushed on the plane and rushed her to the hospital, while I struggled to gather the girls and the luggage to get us to the car. I finally made it to the car and immediately called the girls' godparents, where I dropped them off before heading to the hospital. Fortunately, it was nothing major. It scared the crap out of me because Leslie had a biopsy earlier that month. The doctor had assured us there was nothing to worry about so we didn't, until this happened. Things seemed to regain some sense of normalcy as the New Year began. I left for Arizona the first weekend of the year for work and to run a half marathon. Before I left she asked if we could talk to our Pastor again, and although I didn't see the point, I agreed to it. As I stood in baggage claim having just landed in Arizona, my cell phone rang. I answered and told her that I was just about to call and let her know that I had arrived safely. She was a little quiet at first before saying that she had just returned home from the doctor. I asked if there was something wrong with the girls and she said no it was for me. The next four words she spoke brought me to my knees. *"I have breast cancer!"* I was absolutely devastated. A rush of emotion hit me as if I had stepped into oncoming traffic and been hit by a speeding eighteen-wheeler. I was the pillar of strength on the phone with her but then I called my sister, Melanie (Mel), and lost it. I was supposed to be this dynamic motivational leader of this marathon training program and I am at the back of the bus, crying uncontrollably. The pain of losing my mother at a young age rushed to the surface. "Not again!" I thought. This can't be happening again were words that my sister and I kept saying over and over again. My sister was there every day with our mother so she knew what her life became, and I saw the impact that it had had on Mel at an early age. Would the girls have to grow up without their mother? Their mother didn't deserve this and neither did they. I asked myself, "Was this my fault?" I handled my work responsibilities that weekend and ran the half marathon. I was running in a complete daze and had never felt more alone. As I ran, I was crying on the inside but also felt this calm reassurance that everything was going to be alright. I smiled as I crossed the finished line after 13.1 miles. Although I was going through so much inner turmoil, I felt embraced by some type of security blanket. I would later come to realize that God talks to me when I run and it is the one time that I actually listen. This is another life lesson I have never forgotten, as this realization would serve me well in the coming months and years.

Upon returning home, it was time to deal with reality. I would help my wife get through this breast cancer fight the best way that I knew how, without leading her on concerning our marriage. I will be the first to admit that I did not do a good job of this. My body was there and I did what she needed me to do, but I should have been there more emotionally. Maybe a part of it was my fear that the girls and I would lose her. Maybe it was me trying to be the rock of strength for her and the girls. Maybe it was because I had lost my ability to communicate and be in the moment with her. Maybe I still couldn't handle the emotional toll and devastation that I experienced with the loss of my mother. Whatever the reason, I failed with flying colors and I feel that I will never be able to repay her for that failure. But I am also a believer that you can become a better person in the midst of failure and I would like to think that is what happened for me.

As the year marched on, I was notified that the marathon training program was being shut down nationally, which meant I would be out of a job at the end of the summer. While this was going on, my wife had gotten through her mastectomy, chemotherapy and radiation treatments. Her mother was a big help in assisting with taking care of our home and the kids. Leslie really seemed to be bouncing back and running was the one thing that kept me sane while preventing me from having a nervous breakdown. I ran three more half marathons and a full marathon that year. She wanted to move back to Pennsylvania to be close to her family, and I was fine with that but I would be moving north too as the girls were two and four and I felt I needed to be close to them. I was determined to be a part of their lives. She had a job waiting in Pennsylvania and I secured a job in northern Virginia. I felt that it was important that we discuss custody and divorce before we left but she kept putting it off. I filed divorce papers and had her served. That didn't go over very well and it's honestly not what I preferred, but I wanted to protect my rights as a father. I had heard so many horror stories of divorced parents, and mothers holding their kids hostage not allowing the fathers to be a part of their children's lives. She would never do that and I should have known better, but at the time I just wanted to make sure that my rights were protected as a father. After living in Tampa for over sixteen years, I moved to northern Virginia and my soon to be ex-wife moved to Pennsylvania.

The first time that I went to see the girls I picked them up and we stayed in a hotel. I remember lying in the bed that first night as I listened to the girls breathing deeply as they slept. Had I done the right thing? Was this going to be our existence? The first year we followed the court orders to the letter as far as visitation, and we eventually came to an arrangement where we would alternate the holidays and I could see the girls whenever I wanted. She told me that she would never deny me the opportunity to see my girls because after all, they were my girls. I have always appreciated her for that. I moved to DC and the girls would come and spend part of the summer with me. I would drop them off at camp and I would go to work. One summer we planned on them staying a little longer so that she could take some long-term medical precautions in response to the cancer that was in remission. I eventually got a job in Pennsylvania myself and she let me sleep on the couch for a few weeks until I could find adequate housing. One night we had a long conversation about life and our marriage. We both took ownership for why our marriage had failed and agreed our number one priority was to get our children through this beautiful thing called life. I had always respected her, but I gained an even greater appreciation for her as a strong black woman that night. I knew that I would always love her as the mother of my children, the way that best friends love each other. We will forever be linked by our children, but I feel like our bond is strong because of the life that we have shared both together and apart. I see the mix of both of us in our girls and it just astounds me. The girls see a happy daddy and a happy mommy and we both pray that we will give them great footsteps to follow. The blessings that resulted from love, marriage and divorce are quite simple in this instance. The children that God gave us were our greatest blessing and the blessing of eternal friendship. Yes, I lost a wife and a marriage but I gained a best friend that I would trust with my life. My prayer is that we will be there for our kids, co-parenting, for college graduations, weddings and eventually grandchildren...until death do us part!

ADVERSITY: Breast cancer revisiting my life and afflicting someone I cared for, and a failed marriage.
BLESSING: Being a father to Kennedy and Carter and learning to be a best friend to my ex-wife, Leslie.

# CHAPTER 5

## Humpty Dumpty: Putting My Broken Life Back Together

I GUESS NO one plans on being divorced and single again. I was very fortunate to move to northern Virginia and then Washington, DC. I had a base of friends that I had gone to college with and I would need them during this transition. When I got there, it was almost like a homecoming. Old friends embraced me as if time had stood still since our college days. I wasn't sure how I would like city living, as I have always been a country boy at heart. I can't express how critical it was for me to reconnect with friends at this point in my life. We did everything together. We all went to clubs together, laughed together and cried together. They made me feel like I belonged. I met new people that were so cool and were all about helping each other to be better. The sheer uplift was amazing. Of course, there were my home girls, who wanted to introduce me to their girlfriends and that was cool. My boys that lived outside of the DC area would call and say, "Man, I know you're killing the game in Chocolate City." Truth be told, I wasn't that guy anymore. The partying and the women were something that I left in my youth. I was divorced and single, and I was different. I was a grown-up now and still had some growing to do. My head was not into dating because I told myself I was never, ever getting married again. I wasn't in any rush for a relationship either, as I realized I needed time to heal from my failed marriage. I met some special people during this time that deserved better treatment from me, but only in hindsight did I understand that. At the time, I was oblivious to how they really felt about me because I was taking time for me. When I look back, it was really a case of the right place at the wrong time. I was blind at the time simply because I wasn't ready for anything substantial, even if I gave off that kind of air. My body may have said one thing but my mind said something different. I can only acknowledge these things in retrospect because I am older and wiser than I was then. At the time, I was working on becoming a better version of myself.

My time in DC played an important role in my learning about the true essence of friendship. As a member of the Omega Psi Phi Fraternity, Inc., our motto is *Friendship is Essential to the Soul.* I have to acknowledge that this motto is one of the staples of my existence. In my lifetime, I have had good friends and acquaintances and I have had wolves disguised as friends, and it takes a special skill to differentiate between the two. Unfortunately, we don't always get that one right. I was blessed to grow up with friends from my neighborhood who were real: Kevin, Cil, Redd, Pete and Ronald. We grew up together and although we were different we had each other's back and even more, the neighborhood had our back. When I went to college my frame of reference when it came to friendship was what I grew up knowing. I had to learn the hard way that all friendships aren't the same.

One instance that I learned the hard way was when I was living with three of my teammates in an apartment during my third year of college. One of them, whose career had ended due to an injury, was pretty down on himself and decided he was going to sucker punch me one night. I had been having great success on the football field and my parents and girlfriend were in town to see the game that weekend. Another one of my roommates had a friend visiting from out of town for the weekend. He had gotten really drunk at an on-campus party and passed out. None of my other roommates were around so I took him to the hospital. A couple of them finally showed up at the hospital. As I walked out of the emergency room headed to my car, one of my roommates pushed me in the back. I asked him what he was doing and then continued toward my car. He pushed me again and I asked "What's the problem?" I said that I had to get to the hotel to pick up my girl, who was with my parents. I again turned to walk away only to be pushed again. This time I turned around and the next thing I knew I was picking myself up off the ground. He sucker-punched me and I never saw it coming. I looked to the left and saw the police running out of the emergency room. When I looked straight ahead I saw my two roommates driving away. The police told me that I was just assaulted and asked if I wanted to press charges. I said no and proceeded to walk into the emergency room to get stitches in my lip. I never saw that coming from someone who I thought was a friend. I had done nothing but be a friend to this dude. I called my dad and told him what happened and he was incensed. My recall now is a little hazy but I believe my dad called Kevin, who had moved to Dallas after leaving the military, and Kevin had called the fellas in North Carolina from the old neighborhood. They were all rallying the posse to come to Charlottesville to have a "conversation" with old boy. It took some talking but I convinced them to stand down and assured them I would handle it. My crew was not having it and I will always love them for having my back way back then. The lesson I learned back then was that all friendships are not the same and as much as I thought these guys were like my friends that I grew up with, they were far from it. Then a young man named William Thomas Noel entered my life. We became room-mates and he became like a brother to me. He changed my college experience for the better. I still say that God put him in my life be-cause I sure needed him at that time. We eventually rented a duplex with four bedrooms and our friends Terry Tomlin and Kenny Johnson moved in with us. We called ourselves the Four Horsemen. We still call ourselves that, for the record. As I look back on our time spent together it makes me say, in my best Big Sean voice, "Way up, I feel blessed." The friendships of my late teens and early twenties where very important; however, I really want to focus on the friendships in my adult life that played a vital role when I needed them most.

When I moved to Washington DC, I reconnected with many of my former classmates from college, and though we may not have been that close while we were in school, we became that way once I moved to the DC area. I won't name everyone so I apologize for the omissions in advance. Friends like Nishelle, who allowed me to bunk in a guest room until I found a place of my own. Our daily conversations were extremely impactful. She introduced me to Cathy and the three of us became the three legs of a tripod. We were inseparable. Those ladies were there for me at a critical time in my life. I can never repay them for their friendship. Candice and Charla also come to mind. Our gatherings for spades games and book club were incredible. Assata will always be treasured for her trust and loyalty. I remember so many conversations where we just kept each other's head on straight. We were, and are, kindred spirits. Funmi, the Nigerian teddy bear, will always be loved for her confident and commanding presence, but more importantly for the soft caring person underneath. She would eventually introduce me to my future wife, Ericka. Yes, I know I said that I was never getting married again, but that's the reason one should *never* say **never**. I will always love Michele and David for always welcoming my kids and I into their home and making us feel like family. A few of my fraternity brothers were critical at this time too. Although there are many, some stood out tremendously. I want to give a shout out to Doug Bass, T. Free, Dele, Marvin, Strud, Hopson, Abdul, Corey and Greg. I'm thankful because each was there at least once, if not multiple times, with a shoulder to lean on. Sometimes it was an ear to listen, a 9-hole round of golf, or a chair at their table for a libation. They each had an impact and I thank them for knowing when to be there. I will always remember football Sundays when the entire crew would come over to my spot on Georgia Avenue. Folks would show up around 12:30 pm with their team jerseys on, loaded with food and beverage. Every week we would run out of food close to the 7:30 pm game and we would walk down the block and grab pizzas. People would take naps and then wake up and start up again. This was the family environment that I have always needed in my life and had been missing for a while. When we went to a club, we *all* went to the club. We would always support the events that Doug was associated with and the party didn't start until we got there. We did everything together because we enjoyed being around each other. The best times were always when we met at someone's house though. The thing that made this group so special is that everyone was real. We didn't mind checking each other if there was a need for it, and there just wasn't a bunch of pretentious BS. We had a strong core, and although new people were introduced to the group they would be weeded out for certain gatherings. The group generally had a good feel about these matters even if I was fooled occasionally myself. Oops! Did I write that? I guess we can't always be perfect. A wolf in sheep's clothing is still a wolf though, and there is a lesson to be learned from a wolf too. A wolf teaches you that not everyone is a friend no matter how well they are disguised, and though their bite can leave a deep scar, we must learn to forgive them. They are just creatures that have been scarred themselves and they use sheep's clothing to hide those scars. Besides, God forgave us when He didn't have to, so forgiveness frees us from carrying around the bitterness or bad taste that was left by the betrayal. The lesson that I received and now understand is I've got to go to God before allowing new people into my space. Today, when new people come into my life, I ask God if this is someone that He is bringing into my life and if it is not then please remove them from my life. I want no one in my space that is not put there by God, because they are potential dream takers and I don't need that for me. I know beyond a shadow of a doubt that God has put some incredible people in my life, who enhanced it greatly in DC.

One of the best times that I can remember was when a group of us went to Cabo San Lucas, Mexico to celebrate my 40th birthday. We rented a villa, bought groceries and alcohol and lived like kings and queens. Days were spent by our pool listening to music, talking and drinking tequila. We invaded the town at night for partying and then we would wake up and press repeat. We hit the beach, rode ATV's, (we almost lost Assata compliments of a huge wave as she posed for pictures), shopped, and none of us will ever forget El Squid Row and Club Lord Black. Those places were off the chain. As I sit and reflect about that trip, there were so many comical moments. We even tried to capture them by writing down some of the funny sayings. I sure wish I could remember them today, because we laughed for months after we returned home. T. Free and his crew always had the unique parties where you were assured of having a great time. The Halloween parties were always epic and the house parties weren't far behind them. It was another good crew of people that interestingly enough was about elevating each other. That was one thing about DC that I loved. My different crews of people were progressive black people, who were always trying to help elevate each other. When so many of our people have such a "crabs in a barrel" type of mentality, it was so refreshing watching people of color helping each other. Chocolate City was amazing.

My line brother, Dele, lived less than a mile away so it was great that I had easy access to him. I got him into long distance running and he became a machine. His dog, Ayo, would run with us on Saturday mornings in the Park, whether we ran four miles or ten miles. I still believe to this day that dog was bionic. I'd never seen anything like it. I remember one morning when the temperature was in the twenties and we had a ten-mile run. Ayo was there every step of the way. We got more of our fraternity brothers and friends into running. I vividly remember one Saturday morning, there were about six of us (Dele, Ken, Tone, Javin, Bashon and myself) and we asked each other if we would have ever thought we would all be together years after college, at 6:30 am on a Saturday morning, about to run six miles. We all laughed at the notion and then we got it done. Dele then got me into cycling but the jury is still out on that one. I am thankful for Dele and his family, who have always embraced me. He and I would talk for hours or just sit there in silence and be just as connected. I think that connection stemmed from our pledge process so many years ago. We were very connected during our process and although we missed quite a few years together when I lived in Florida, the bond always remained. When we reconnected with my move to the DC area, it was as if no time had passed at all. He is also the best storyteller, ever. There is nothing like a road trip when he tells you a story of an encounter that he has had. It always promises to be epic, believe you, me. He is accomplished, educated, and opinionated and he is a man that I would trust with my life. I'm so thankful that God put him in my life over 27 years ago. We have kept each other going through our support for one another. We have had to put our foot in each other's behind at one time or another to stay focused and on track. My children call him Uncle Dele and they love and respect him. That started fairly early in their lives because of the man himself and his authentic nature. One time Kennedy, my oldest, had an issue at school and I told him about it. Now my girls and I love to go to the movies but on this particular weekend, Kennedy would not go to the movies with Carter and me. Instead, she went over to Uncle Dele's as a part of her discipline. Carter and I had a great time at the movies and then we went and picked up Kennedy. When we arrived, and walked in the backyard, we saw her helping with yard work. She put the last of the leaves in a garbage bag that Dele was holding and took the gloves off and walk towards us. Dele called her back and gave her a firm, "Now you know you have to stay focused in school and we won't have to worry about this again, will we?" She said, "No" and he gave her a zip locked bag of cookies and told her that he loved her. She hugged him and ran over to me. I winked at him and said, "Thanks Bruh." Then there was the time the girls and I were hanging out over there and Carter was walking towards the truck near the garage when she tripped on the step and hit her chin on the pavement. She was crying hysterically and blood was all over. I picked her and we ran back inside. He, I and his wife Robin got her all cleaned up and calmed down. There was just something about the way that he spoke to her though. She felt the safety of my arms around her but she also felt the love of her Uncle Dele. Their love and respect for him is unwavering, even though they don't see him as much. I knew that he would become a great father when his time came and now that he has two children of his own, greatness has been delivered. I was introduced to another fraternity brother named Abdul. They don't make good brothers like him anymore. We were both from the same home state of North Carolina. We shared our life stories with one another and had quite a few similarities. It is funny how you find out who your true friends are when you go through adversity. These are the lifelong friends that show up or call just to check on you, just because. They have nothing to gain but you have impacted them in some way and they genuinely care about how you're doing. Friendship has always been very important to me throughout my life. As I stated earlier, I grew up with good friends and I have been stabbed in the back by people that I thought were friends. At the end of the day, friendship will always be one of the ties that bind me. God has blessed me with some incredible people in my lifetime, both good and bad. I have learned from them both and I am thankful that in my darkest hours, God has put the right people there at the right time. So many people were placed in my path during a critical time in my life and I know that could only be His Grace. I can only pray that I have been able to positively impact the lives of my friends the way that they have impacted mine. My chapter brother Doug once told me that before I moved back to the area that the crew hung out sometimes, but for the most part, they did their own thing. When I moved to the area, I was able to bring everyone together. He told me that I was the glue. I will never forget that because it gives affirmation that as much as I felt that they were all a blessing to me, I too was able to bless them with the gift of true friendship.

ADVERSITY: Struggling to rebuild my life and become a better version of myself.
BLESSING: Discovering an abundance of God-given friendships.

# CHAPTER 6

## Life of Service

A LIFE OF service is a trait that I must have inherited from my mother. She was always so giving of her time and money, even when she didn't have it to give. It used to tick me off. Today I have to laugh, because I am just like her. I too have given my time and money to friends or people in need. I've volunteered and worked serving others in the non-profit space for over sixteen years. Working for non-profit organizations was never my plan but it seemed to just happen organically. It's almost as if the non-profit world found me. My first service opportunity occurred in 2000 for a well-known organization. I interviewed for one position, but ended up being hired for another one. They wanted me to lead their efforts in a pilot program called *Train to End Stroke* (TTES), which was designed to raise money for stroke research and education. They told me upfront that they hadn't done a program like this before nor did they have anyone to teach me. They just handed me a manual, gave me a pat on the back and told me to make it happen. It was a tremendous challenge, but I was game.

During that pilot season, I followed the manual for the most part but made some subtle tweaks to it that made sense to me. The basic premise was that people would respond to a mailing inviting them to attend a meeting to find out how they could go to an exotic location, raise money for a great cause and learn more about strokes and heart disease. Once they came to the meeting, we showed them how they could both raise money and complete a half or full marathon in a very desirable location. What I didn't know was just how prevalent strokes were, and how devastating they could be on so many different communities. With all of this new-found education on strokes and heart disease it became imperative for me to get this information out to the masses. This was so different from selling water treatment equipment. I was now educating and motivating people to affect change. This seemed like life-saving work, like work that was going to move the needle and really change lives. I no idea how much this work would impact me, personally, but it felt like the place I was always destined to be with a sense of purpose. We trained a group of individuals and took them to Hawaii to participate in the Kona Marathon. It was a life changing experience for me. I witnessed people from around the country attempting something that most of them never imagined they could accomplish. Most of them participated in memory or in honor of a friend or family member who had suffered a stroke. We also had some stroke survivors who completed the marathon. My heart was full after bearing witness to their selfless acts of courage. I left Hawaii a changed man, motivated to grow the program. I wanted to share my testimonial with anyone who would listen, and let them know they had the power to change lives. I engaged people with one simple question, "If it was in your power to save a life, would you?" I also decided that if I was going to ask people to raise money and complete a half or full marathon then I needed to be willing to do so myself. I too would raise money and train to participate. I was truly putting my money where my mouth was. So, I trained with my participants and raised money to run in the Disney Marathon. It was extremely challenging, and one of the more gratifying things I had ever done because it wasn't about me. I knew that I was running on behalf of the stroke survivors with whom I had come in contact. I was running for Ray, for Helen, for Patti and the dozens of survivors who had touched my life. They were my driving force when I was cramping at mile 22 along with a will that had been there all of my life. A will that had helped me overcome, persevere, and never quit. When that medal was placed around my neck after crossing the finish line, I felt like I was walking on cloud nine with even more determination to grow the program. Ultimately, I was able to expand the program to Fort Lauderdale and Orlando and build out a team. I hired a spunky and fiery young lady named Leah to head the Ft. Lauderdale market, and after one season in Orlando I was able to recruit Denise from Minnesota, who was a part of the original pilot season, to come and run the Orlando team. I had added two more locations to the Tampa market. My team was working well and we were growing. One of the most amazing things about the work was the lives that we impacted. Our participants viewed us like family and we felt the same way about them. I became close with so many stroke survivors, who invited me to speak at their stroke survivor conferences. I was always amazed at how they would wait in line to talk to me. They would tell me that they felt like I understood them and that was always so moving for me. I realized I could inspire and motivate people in a different way. I have always been a passionate and fairly intense person, but this was different. The experience taught me how to uplift people by believing in them and letting them know they could overcome tough challenges if they just believed in themselves. By sharing a part of my life and my experiences I was able to give them a glimmer of hope. I was their biggest cheerleader and they knew it. I sometimes ran alongside them just to show them that I believed in them and sometimes that's all that was needed. They changed me as much as I changed them and showed me that perspective can sometimes come in the strangest places. Our little program grew from just a manual to locations in Tampa, Orlando, Ft. Lauderdale, West Palm Beach, Miami and Jacksonville. The job was a grind and non-stop, but to those of us who stuck it out, it was worth it. Zach B, Smitty and the Boston crew, as well Kendra, Heidi, Rebecca and so many great staff from across the country—they all poured their hearts into the program to make it become successful. Our program in Florida was one of the top performing affiliates in the country. We developed our own best practices, our own strategy and occasionally we went outside of the national parameters because it positioned us to be successful. The National office had their ideas of how they thought the program should be run, but it was us, the splendid foot soldiers, who knew the inner workings of how to move the machine forward. In fact, we helped some affiliates get back on their feet as a result of past struggles. We became a model program for how to recruit, retain and excel. While I will take some credit for designing strategy, I had a great team around me. Everyone from Denise, to Leah, to Big Tex, to Adrienne, to Robyn, to Maria, to Buck, to Liz and all of our coaches and volunteers and staff that are too many to name. My Florida team and other partner affiliates came together to guide the ship. If the national office would have allowed the people in the field to guide the national approach, I am certain the overall program would have been sustainable. Unfortunately, the national office handcuffed the affiliates by making decisions that eventually crippled the program making it too cost prohibitive for the affiliates. After six years of positive growth, my boss called me in the office and told me that they were going to follow the national office's lead and shut down the program. It was a crushing blow. The team was devastated and our TTES family was equally crushed. The outpouring of letters, emails and phone calls asking what, if anything, could be done to save the program was overwhelming. There was so much love out there for this program and I learned a lot. I learned how to become an effective manager from my boss,

Chuck T., who always laid out the expectations and trusted me to go out and get the job done. I learned how to hold people accountable and how to navigate internal politics from my co-worker, Bali, who is still my best friend today. She has always been one of the most polished and buttoned up women with whom I have had the pleasure to work. Her loyalty has been unwavering and is more like a sister than a friend. I learned how to design strategy, to teach a selling style, to be innovative and to take risks. I learned that I was a master at networking and building relationships. I learned that I could start a program and build it from the ground up and make it successful. I learned that I could be an agent for change and that I could empower others to do great things. I took all of these things away from that experience. I assumed all non-profits worked this way and I was hooked. I was also wrong...very wrong.

Over the next two to three years I worked for a couple of different non-profits. Having built out a strong work history and resume, I was being recruited. The first opportunity landed me in northern Virginia with a non-profit that wanted to build a development department, or at least they thought they did. I was there for a couple of years and did some good things, but it wasn't a permanent destination. I made some great connections with world renowned physicians, yet I knew that it was time to make a move when one of them told me she felt the organization was not really willing to grow as fast as they said they were, and that while they talked a good game about being ready to grow and expand, it was really just lip service. I always appreciated her for being honest with me and I made sure that I had a bottle of Chardonnay for her whenever I saw her, as it was her favorite. I was fortunate enough to call a select group of these physicians, friend. Val Jackson, Bruce Hillman and Bill Bradley were among my favorite physicians.

I was then recruited by an organization based in Bethesda, Maryland that was focused on raising money for childhood cancer research. It was an opportunity to get back to the mission-driven work I grew to love working with TTES, and back to working, hands-on, with the people for whom the money raised would directly benefit. I interviewed for the job and it sounded like an awesome opportunity. They did a great job of selling the job and the salary was very respectable. It proved to be one of the worst job decisions I ever made. They talked about having a huge donor base and all of these resources to help me be successful. They too had some "renowned" physicians who, I was told, I would have at my disposal. My first week on the job, the Executive Director approached me and said she wanted me to cold call a list of twenty-five Fortune 500 companies. I would like to think I was pretty darn good at my job, but not special enough to cold call into the likes of Target and Wal-Mart, to name a few, and think I was going to reach the decision maker. The non-profit game doesn't work that way. That was the first red flag. It became a virtual revolving door of development staff. After being there only six months, I was the longest tenured development person. It was clear that my boss was out of her depth. That was the second and third red flags. Then I heard that the executive board attempted to get rid of her before I got there, but she found out about it and threatened a lawsuit. Meanwhile, the "renowned" physicians sat on their hands and were not very helpful. We weren't bringing in any money so they hired a new President and CEO. I met with him, shared the challenges, and my belief that we could rebound with an appropriate strategy. He seemed very interested in working to help develop that strategy. Within a month or less his entire attitude had changed. I was called into a meeting in which my boss had thrown me under the bus so badly that I never thought I would get the tire prints off of my body. She was in a free fall trying to save her job and was going to say or do anything to anyone to that end. I was let go after only 10 months, as the new CEO brought in his own team. Incidentally, my former boss was relieved of her duties, shortly thereafter. Man, God doesn't like ugly and karma is real. I learned how NOT to run a development department there, which proved a valuable experience.

I was then approached about an opportunity in Philadelphia. It would be a challenge, as it had been a flourishing program in years past, but had been in a downward spiral for quite some time. I was told by some of the executive leadership at the national office in Washington, DC that Philadelphia was the number one priority for them because it was a program in a major market that was consistently failing. When I was initially approached about the opportunity, I was intrigued because I do love a challenge and I saw the greater opportunity to work for the national office in DC if I could successfully rebuild the Philadelphia market. However, I did say no to the initial offer because, quite honestly, the salary was too low. The President and CEO then came back with more money by realigning some staffing priorities. Translation: he combined the development and program director positions into one job. I had experience in both areas so it made sense and it was a good move on his part. In hindsight, I should have asked him to combine the full salary for both positions. If I knew then what I know now after going through the experience, I would have demanded it. But hey money isn't everything, right? It was an opportunity to be in the same city as my daughters and I countered his offer with a $5,000 **net** "signing" bonus. He agreed but said that we couldn't call it a "signing" bonus. I have no idea why but I took the job and moved to Philadelphia. The first red flag was when I received the "signing" bonus; taxes had been taken out of it lowering the net amount below what was agreed upon. Here's my issue...if we make an agreement on a bonus of $5,000 **net**, then the gross of what's given has to be higher in order to meet the $5,000 net number. Simple accounting principles, right? I called the President and CEO and asked him about it and he said that he misunderstood what we agreed upon. What's funny is that he agreed to it in writing, but I just let it go. I questioned his character from that point on. A man's word should be his bond, especially when it's in writing.

The program was an absolute mess, which meant I had to get to work fast. There were only about 300 hundred athletes in the program, which was a damn Greek tragedy considering Philadelphia's major metropolitan status. A lot of people didn't really know that there was a local chapter of the organization with local games. The local chapter also had limited money and limited resources. One of the best things that happened initially was that I was given the opportunity to work with an awesome sports director, Michelle. She had all of the institutional knowledge and was truly a godsend for me. She was immensely talented and grossly under appreciated by the state office. We were a two-person team for a broken program that needed a major overhaul. My boss and the President and CEO shared the business plan with me, which read well on paper, but in reality, needed some serious work. I decided to focus on three major areas: athlete recruitment, marketing and fundraising. I wanted Michelle to stay focused on the sports aspect of things because that was her strength, and I would pick her brain for other areas, if necessary. We didn't have a relationship with the school district, which definitely affected the recruitment of our athletes. I immediately worked to repair that relationship. We had a liaison, Alton, and he and I hit it off right out of the gate. He was my internal advocate at the school district. I met with anyone in the school district who was willing to meet. What really got things going was when I attended a school nurses meeting and one of the school nurses said his school had a sports program that was working with kids with special needs. He later set up a meeting with me at the school, and soon thereafter, we started programming there. It wasn't exactly a blueprint for how to start a program, but you have to be able to adapt and "get in where you fit in". Once it got going, it started growing fairly quickly. As I mentioned, I inherited a little over 300 athletes in all of Philadelphia and within the first year between our school-based and community-based programs, we had grown to over 700 athletes. I then turned to marketing and fundraising. I was convinced that if people knew about us they would support us. I needed to create some strategic partnerships. I created a Council of Trustees, who would serve as my board. I selected four movers and shakers in the city, who all had connections. Two of them had children with special needs so they were very passionate partners, and the other two were change agents who believed in my passion and wanted me to be successful. Their companies supported us financially and opened doors to a media partnership as well as other relationships. I was able to have my athletes interviewed on television, as well as getting local media coverage at our various events around the city. I developed a signature event that exceeded goal in its first year and was attended by the Interim School Superintendent at the time, as well as a member of the Philadelphia Eagles, the Eagles cheerleaders, the Temple women's basketball team and many, many others. It was a very successful event, and brought a needed team atmosphere to this program. We had jerseys and t-shirts printed with "T.E.A.M. PHILLY". The athletes and parents loved it. In fact, there were two comments that I will never forget receiving from a couple of parents. One parent told me that she "really appreciated me attending so many of their events because they weren't used to having someone at the director level there." I told her that these kids are my T.E.A.M. Another parent thanked me for bringing my daughters to the events and letting them interact with the athletes. "It means the world to us as parents and to the athletes." I will forever be moved by their kind words. I was able to repair so many hard feelings the parents felt towards the state office and those in power. I did that by being in the moment and by not just showing up when the camera was there. I understood that the program was about the athletes and it wasn't a stage for those with the big paycheck, suit and tie and poked out chest, as if they had been there all along. I understood that this was God's work and not man's time for celebrating what he had or had not done.

I had done so much work to rebuild this program, that my work was acknowledged by some of the national and international officers when they came to Philadelphia for a meeting with the leadership of the school district. The School District personnel raved about all the work I had done and our visitors from headquarters stated that they knew that the right man was hired for the job. I was honored and told that they would support whatever needs this program encountered. None of us knew that I would be facing an internal attack within our own staff. My biggest mistake was a lack of willingness to agree with every decision from the state office when it came down to the local program. I'm the kind of guy that wouldn't want a bunch of "yes men" around me. Just give me the truth and nothing but the truth. I disagreed with the state office on a couple of issues for which I felt the local office would not be able to deliver. I had my hand on the pulse of what was going on in Philadelphia and I knew our shortcomings and our bandwidth. My predecessor, on the other hand, had been previously embarrassed by having to return money that was not utilized due to bandwidth issues. I did not want to be embarrassed the same way. Ultimately, a plan was conceived to force me out. I was blindsided one day when I went to the state office to have a discussion about the budget for the upcoming fiscal year. At that meeting, I was given a letter that my performance needed improvement but was given no deliverables on what I was supposed to do to improve. They even had the gall to question my leadership. I was stunned, but gathered myself and took the council of a fraternity brother on how I should respond. My chapter brother Kevin Best (KB) was instrumental in helping me work through this. I responded with my own set of deliverables. I would show them how ridiculous it was to question my ability when I had brought the program back from the ashes like a phoenix. My deliverables were challenging and I set a timeline of 30-60 days. I completed every single one. Unfortunately, it was a waste of time because the decision had already been made before they gave me the initial letter. This was a machination that was Machiavellian in nature. They wanted me to call it a resignation because they knew parents, volunteers and sponsors would not be happy to learn of my termination. They knew people would wonder why they would get rid of me after I had brought a program out of the ashes. They were unwilling to fight that battle. They kept me on for a couple more weeks and offered me a severance package provided I declared my departure a resignation and agreed to surrender to them my contacts. Yes—the contacts I had spent countless hours developing after business hours, while they were home with their families enjoying their lives. I agreed to their conditions. Frankly, because I needed my paycheck, I had to do what I had to do. What's interesting is that they really believed they could maintain those relationships without me. Instead, they failed miserably, as they lost Council of Trustee members and other key sponsors. What they failed to realize is that people give to people they like, and that likability factor is built through genuine relationship development over time. They would never be able to replicate my unique passion for the mission nor my ability to connect with people. Several months after my departure, a sponsor I had cultivated called me to catch up and shared a very interesting observation. He said the President and CEO "realized you didn't need him to be successful leading the program, but that he couldn't do it without you." He went on to explain that "once you rebuilt the program he thought he could just plug someone else in there to do the job with the same lack of resources with which you had been saddled with. He had no idea how to deal with the urban market in Philadelphia. He was going to use your work as a feather in his cap for greater self-gain." Similar observations had run through my mind before, but it was reassuring and sad at the same time to have them validated by someone else. In my gut, I knew the guy never really valued me because of a question he once asked me in the midst of a fund-raiser. He asked, "How is that we have so much going on now? We have the school superintendent on board, our athlete numbers are up and people know about us. What's different?" I looked at him and said, "You added me." In hindsight, that may have been an arrogant thing to say but it was the truth, and even though the truth hurts sometimes that doesn't diminish its validity. The fact that he didn't understand how hard that I had worked spoke volumes about his disconnection from the truth. To be honest, I survived that job experience because of Michelle, the athletes, parents and volunteers. Even though I survived it, my love for non-profit work was significantly damaged. But like Al Pacino said in Godfather III, "Just when I thought I was out, they pull me back in." The non-profit game pulled me back in again.

My next two opportunities were in Washington, DC and Baltimore. Both organizations struggled at various levels of leadership. The DC experience was disappointing because I expected better from the organization. It was an organization with a tremendous historic brand that had lost its way, with no strategy for how to move it forward at any level. I studied a five-year fundraising trend when I first arrived, which revealed every phase of development had been trending downward with no plan other than to continue with the definition of insanity—keep doing the same thing while expecting a different result. I had a supervisor who had a mad hustle game, but was not very polished. I often wondered why in the hell she was in a supervisory role after witnessing her burn more bridges than a raging fire and talk to leadership in a manner that left me shaking my head. "She must truly know where the bones are buried" I speculated. She was loud, adversarial and not really well thought of around the office or in the broader development community, for that matter. Don't shoot the messenger. I'm just telling the unsolicited word on the street. There also was a revolving door at this organization, through which a lot of talented people cycled in and out. Many of those who remained were just biding their time until another opportunity presented itself. During my tenure there, I may have seen 10-15 people leave for other jobs, until one day I too left for another job. Though my tenure there was brief, I left with long standing friendships with a handful of people with whom I really enjoyed working, and a lot of connections in the Baltimore market I developed through a very successful Mayor's Luncheon. These benefits would bode well for me as I transitioned to a position in Baltimore.

I was very hopeful for the Baltimore opportunity but quickly realized it was hampered by very limited resources. Again, there were some really good people there, who I enjoyed working with, but turnover was an all too familiar issue. Some left for better opportunities because they had been passed over for internal advancement or because they hated both the leadership and direction, or lack thereof, of the organization. The organization's leadership was definitely questionable and there was no strategic plan whatsoever. Promises were made and then not delivered, which would become a recurring theme. I was promised a bonus structure to get my salary to a level that was at least manageable, for me. It wasn't developed in the first year. I tried my hardest to understand their health benefits before I accepted the job, but ran into roadblock after roadblock trying to ascertain costs. I should've known better than to take the job before all of that was clear. After my second week on the job I finally received the health insurance costs for my daughters and I. They were astronomical. I immediately went to the President and CEO and told him that I couldn't afford the benefits. He looked me right in the face and said, "What do you want me to do? I can't help you." I told him I just wanted to make him aware of my concerns. Then I calmly walked back to my office and started firing out resumes. He unknowingly told me a lot about himself through that encounter. About a week later, our office manager, Debbie, informed me that she had just found out from the healthcare provider that because my daughters lived out of state they were ineligible for healthcare through the company. She then informed the President and CEO, who then called me into his office to discuss the issue. He assured me we would get through this together and that he would call the CEO in Pennsylvania and see if we could "work something out." He never brought it up again. I'm going to go out on a limb and say he never made that call. It was one of many untruths that he would tell during my time there. He was a master of alternative facts. Thank goodness, I had already started searching for healthcare alternatives for my girls. The Affordable Care Act would have to be the alternative and I would be stroking them a big check for three hundred dollars each month. You heard me right... I was paying three hundred dollars a month from my take home pay, but the girls had to have healthcare so I had no choice. I filed that away and went about my job, because at least I had a job, right? I was given the budget and goals for the year and after examining it I realized we needed the help from the board to come close to balancing a budget that was way out of proportion. I expressed my thoughts to the board on how they could be utilized to obtain new business. I heard nothing from them. During my first board meeting I laid out a strategy to secure new corporate business partners and how the board could play a role in that. I challenged them to do more. It seemingly fell on deaf ears. Every board meeting proved to be a mastery of minimalism. There were just too many chiefs and not nearly enough Indians. I would look across at my co-worker, Chris, who oversaw the individual/major giving and just shake my head. Chris would endure some backstabbing, while at the organization, from the CEO who was allegedly his friend. With friends like that, who needs enemies! Chris was eventually forced out, but in all honesty, he was never set up for success. None of us were, for that matter.

With the departure of Chris, all of his responsibilities were dumped in my lap since there was no one else. The CEO wanted me to do the work of two development directors and didn't want to pay me any more money. Wait, I think I've seen this movie before. It wasn't going to happen on my watch. I fought for more money and I put together a bonus structure that made sense. We eventually settled on a fourteen percent pay increase. Honestly, the increase was only about ten percent, because of the "whack" healthcare situation. I fought for the extra percentages to offset what I was paying for healthcare for my kids. The bonus structure was sound, but it was unobtainable based on a budget that proposed increases at a minimum of twenty-eight percent across the board in every area of funding, especially when every area of fund development had decreased in the last three years. I went about the business of putting together an overall fund development strategy since there wasn't a blueprint for me to follow. I sat in board meeting after board meeting listening to numbers that were littered with "funny" math. I sat there in amazement at how a Rembrandt was being painted disguised as competence, when in reality the organization was being lead by a person that couldn't even paint. This was a classic case of perception not meeting reality. The clear indication should have been seen through the big glass window of a failing organization, but it wasn't and I just couldn't do it anymore.

One of my co-workers and I decided to meet with three board members, who we felt were really in tune with what was going on. We asked them what they thought of the organization. We talked about the struggles of the organization and the high turnover of staff. We talked about the absence of an overall strategic plan for the organization that needed to have been presented from our leader. As the meeting concluded, I was asked if our CEO was the man to lead the organization. I looked out the window, and then told him that my co-worker and I are here to help move the organization in the right direction. I chose not to throw the guy under the bus, though I could have. I didn't need to because they already knew. They had gotten him CEO coaching and they were hiring a chief of staff to support him. However, if we were an organization struggling to make payroll each month, how were they going to hire a chief of staff? I don't believe the CEO coaching ever worked. This guy's ego would not allow him to be coached. He possessed the gift of gab and could spin a story and make anyone believe it, but he had burned so many bridges in the city and word around town in the corporate space was that he was toxic. Why couldn't the board see this? It was truly a head scratcher. More key people left the organization and more people were terminated to free up resources for the new chief of staff. The

CEO was riding high not realizing that the new Chief of Staff would be groomed to be his replacement. When she came on board she asked me if I was happy at the organization. She said that I didn't look happy. I told her that I was tired. Truth be told, I was mentally drained and hated coming to work. I was tired of the untruths and the lack of resources. People have always gravitated to me for my leadership, but sometimes there is a realization that you cannot always be the leader. Any good leader knows that sometimes he must follow. Though, it is difficult for a good leader to follow poor leadership. I tried to stay the course, because I wanted to try to fix what I could before I left the place. Plus, the cycle would only continue to repeat itself if I didn't put some strategy in place for the next person. I got a call from a friend one day about an opportunity with another organization and she wanted me to meet with a man who I highly respected. I told her flat out that I was done with non-profit work after the crazy place where I was currently working, but she persisted and I eventually agreed to talk with him just because of who it was. I met with him and told him that I didn't plan to do anymore non-profit work and explained to him exactly why I felt the way that I did. I thanked him for the informative conversation about his organization and I left that meeting thinking that was the end of it. I got a call about three weeks later requesting a second interview, which caught me off guard, I must admit. The day before that second interview, I was called into the CEO's office and was laid off. I left the office a bit stunned, but not surprised. It made perfect sense. His plan was to get rid of all the higher salaries and try to fix things with low paid staff and consultants. That is the classic mindset of a person in a position of control that is out of their depth while perceiving themselves to be a leader without the knowledge of how to lead. It's hard for competent people to follow someone that is guiding them towards failure and clearly not possessing the ability to develop a strategic plan to save the organization. I went to my second interview the next day and was hired three weeks later.

The day after I was laid off I spoke with a board member, who told me the organization had done me a favor by letting me go, because I had received a lifeboat from a sinking ship. He told me that even if Michael Jordan was put on a bad team, he would struggle to find success. I won't ever forget that. We recently met for lunch and he was so happy to learn I was flourishing with my new organization. He said it was crazy how all of the people that are no longer with the organization are with other great organizations and are doing so well. He said that it was a shame that all of that talent under one roof was squandered because of the lack of leadership. By the way, the CEO has since been fired and the Chief of Staff is now the President and CEO. Damn, I called that one from day one. It seems he never saw it coming. I guess it goes to show you can't just treat people any kind of way and not expect it to come back to bite you. I believe that is called karma. I pray that he and his family are taken care of and that he finds employment, for it is not my nature to wish ill will on anyone. That's just not how my mama raised me.

ADVERSITY: Losing my job for reasons that were out of my control. BLESSINGS: Positively impacting the lives of so many people with my work, and realizing my God-given gifts to inspire, motivate and build relationships.

# CHAPTER 7

## Coaching and Mentoring

I HAVE TO give credit to coaching football as an important part of shaping me as a man and opening up my perspective on life. Coaching football taught me how to deal with different types of individuals and it gave me the understanding that everyone's situation is different. There is no cookie cutter process in dealing with kids, whether they are from the inner city, the suburbs or from rural areas, everyone has a story. Therefore, a book cannot and should not be judged by its cover. I realized that it is possible to have a positive impact on athletes and kid's, in general, by showing them you genuinely care about them. Gaining their trust is not always easy because a lot of their relationships have lacked trust. Friends have let them down and parents have let them down too. Parenting is not easy and sometimes we don't always get it right. Sometimes mom or dad is holding down two or three jobs just trying to make ends meet, forcing their kids to grow up way faster than they should. A lot of the situations that I dealt with were single parent situations in the inner city. Sometimes these kids just needed to know that someone cared and believed in them. Sports have always been a great outlet for kids to gain confidence and learn about teamwork. A lot of them gain a feeling of belonging and acceptance from it as well. They learn the thrill of victory and the agony of defeat, and one can only hope that sports helps to prepare them for how to deal with the challenges life is sure to present. When I first became a coach, I didn't realize how important a role sports played in teaching life lessons. I knew the game and I knew how to work hard to attain goals. Discipline, conditioning, structure and execution are the keys to winning, at least that's what I thought at the time. I had some success coaching little league with that game plan. I must have the formula, right? I was wrong, but didn't really realize it until I started coaching high school football. The first lesson I had to learn was that every kid is different. Every kid cannot be coached the same way because there are different circumstances in each kid's life. There is no one cookie cutter approach that fits all kids. Life is different for a kid who lives in the inner city versus one who lives in the suburbs, although a different set of issues exists with both. Life appears to be different for a kid who has a stable two-parent household versus a single-parent household. In some of those cases, I noticed that there was not the same level of stability. It really did depend on the parent. I didn't become a good coach until I understood how important it was to figure that out.

We had a great coaching staff of a few former NFL players mixed with some guys who had been successful high school coaches. Our knowledge of the X's and O's was unmatched. We came together from other high school programs in the county with the shared goal of wanting to make a difference in the lives of young men. Some of us had coached with one another and some of us had coached against each other. But we were like-minded in that we wanted to win, had incredible football IQ and cared about the well-being of the kids. We had some good players, but we lacked discipline. Even with the talent that we had, we were average. There was also dissention on the coaching staff, so it was damn near impossible to get the kids on the same page when the coaches weren't on the same page. This became more about managing personalities and egos than about coaching. But that too is a part of coaching. There were some star athletes in the school that were ineligible to play because of issues with their grades. As I got to know these kids, I became more than just a coach to them. I became the person they could talk to and count on.  As I migrated to another inner-city school to coach with my former teammate, Ricky Reynolds, I took on that mentoring role more and more.  It became very important for me to want these kids to not only be successful in sports, but successful outside of sports.  I wanted to teach them how to use the sport to further their education.  I took several of them under my wing, and I was transparent right from the beginning with them.  I told them there would be accountability in the classroom and their teachers would have my cell phone number to keep me apprised of their performance.  And I would be going to parent/teacher conferences.  We would go to church and I would expose them to different things, culturally.  If rules were broken, then there would be consequence to follow at football practice.  None of them wanted that because, in addition to coaching the offense, I was also in charge of strength and conditioning and we were always in the best condition.  The consequence for infractions for academic and football related issues was truly cringe worthy.  I really became like a surrogate father/mentor to a lot of the guys.  I clothed some of these young men when they didn't have clothes to wear.  If I took them to an event where they needed to wear a suit and tie, then I dressed them up and gave them a tie if they needed one.  I taught them how to shake hands and look a person in the eyes when they talked to them.  I took them to movies and sometimes they spent the night at my house.  I even attended advanced placement seminars on Saturday mornings by myself, because I was looking for every angle to get these kids into college in case sports let them down.  Leslie, my wife at the time, even helped one of my guys study for the SAT test at our home.  I gave so much of myself and I honestly lost more kids than I saved, because ultimately, I had to take them home.  I had to take them back to the projects or to homes where the parenting left something to be desired.  They battled with poverty and a sense of hopelessness because of the situations that existed for them at the time. I would always tell them that their current situation was not the end but the beginning and should be used as a stepping-stone to their future. But the reality was that I was battling against the evils of their environment, and while I provided some bright light in the midst of the darkness, it was not bright enough to illuminate the path when I wasn't there.

A classic example of their reality is when I went to pick up one of my guys from the housing projects where he lived. I knocked on the front door and walked inside only to be engulfed with the smoke from his mother smoking marijuana sitting on the couch. I asked where he was and she said upstairs. I go to his room and there were mattresses on the floor in each corner of the room along with garbage bags full of clothes that served as dresser drawers. As we left the house, the drug boys were on the corner with the nice cars and flashy jewelry. That was his reality, and what I had to fight against. Then there were the phone calls I'd receive asking if I would meet one of my guys at the courthouse, because they had to appear before a judge for getting into trouble for doing one of a number of silly teenager things. I remember asking one young man if his mother was meeting us at the courthouse and he said, "No, that's why I called you." As I stood beside him the judge asked who I was and I told him I was his mentor and high school football coach. I told him that I would make sure I kept my foot on his neck and in order to keep him on the right path. Then there was the one student for whom I really had high hopes. He was one of the best high school athletes I had ever seen, but he struggled in the classroom. I really took to him because I saw something in him. He had a fun-loving personality and I felt he just needed someone standing behind him willing to give him that push he so desperately needed. After a lot of work with him, we finally got him scholastically eligible to participate in high school sports again. He eventually moved to Nebraska to finish his high school career, where I heard he had some success. I tried to stay connected to him but we lost touch after a while. Unfortunately, I later heard he came back to Tampa and got into drugs. He spent time in jail and when he got out; someone walked up to him and shot him dead. I was crushed when I found out. Another light dimmed because there just weren't enough positive people in his life pushing him towards a better life. I remember his smile and I remember our conversations to this day. He had a greatness trapped inside and I desperately wanted to help him find it and unleash it. Leslie asked me why I gave so much of myself to these young boys when they were only going to break my heart. "Because I only know how to give them all of me and no one else has ever given them that before," I told her.

As I moved on to coach at a private school the results were different. We inherited a team that had won a total of three to four games in their last couple of seasons combined. They had far less collective talent, but they were hungry to win, worked hard and were committed. It was amazing to watch a well-coached, disciplined team have immediate success. They believed in what we taught them and they saw the fruits of their labor each and every week. What they lacked in talent, they made up for in heart. The first year we won six games and went to the state playoffs. For the next two seasons, we won more than ten games each year and went to the state playoffs. One year we lost in the third round of the state playoffs and the next year we were playing in the state championship game. How did we turn around a program that quickly, you ask? It took a lot of blood, sweat and tears. It took the dedication of the coaches, players, parents and school administrators. It was truly a team effort. As a coaching staff, we out coached many an opposing team. Our kids refused to be outworked because that's how we trained them. It started in the winter and it never stopped. The parents were always there to support the team and the staff. They trusted us with their children because they were a part of the process. Parent involvement proved a major difference in our chemistry with this team and previous teams. Sure, we had a different set of challenges and I still mentored, but the parents were an active part of the equation.

There is nothing like the relationship between a player and a coach where there is genuine trust between the two. There is so much time spent together that in a lot of situations a coach can't help but become somewhat of a surrogate father. I was very close to my high school coaches and although my college head coach wasn't the most personable, I would have run through a wall for him. I was extremely close to my strength and conditioning coach in college. He had a tremendous impact on me, not only as a player, but also in helping me to become a man. When I coached at inner city schools there was often an absence of a father at home a majority of the time, while the private school kids had the benefit of a two-parent home most of the time. I just wanted to see my guys excel and a lot of them went on to college. I still talk to some of them to this very day.

One of my favorite student-athletes was Joey. He was a great kid and was blessed to come from a great family. I will always love that kid. He is the kind of kid a coach dreams of coaching. While Joey was very talented, he worked at being great. He wasn't the fastest receiver but his football IQ was off the charts and he just flat out made the key plays. As practice was winding down one day, I remember Joey asking me if I could show him how to "get off my jam" at the line of scrimmage. We called that "jamming" someone. The back story for that is from doing one-on-one drills with the defensive backs versus the wide receivers. As the defensive backs coach, I would always lead off the one-on-one drill versus a receiver. I would absolutely crush them with my press technique at the line. He was convinced that if he could "get off of *my* jam" then no high school player could stop him. You see, my ability to press the young guys at the line was still pretty impressive for an old man. We went to work after practice as often as he wanted to get some extra work. No newspapers, no cameras or people watching. We just put in the work. I talked him through releases and understanding how to use the field to his advantage. I taught him how to understand the thought process of a defensive back and to never allow them to force him to go where they wanted him to go. Joey absorbed my instruction like a sponge, and on Friday nights, when he would execute something that we worked on, he would come to the sideline and say, "Did you see what I just did to that kid? It was just like we practiced." I was so proud of him because he had demonstrated that if you work hard at something, you will indeed see the fruits of that labor. It reminded me of the many proud moments I shared with my mom and dad. He and I had a special bond and still have one to this very day, even though we don't talk as often as I'd like. But he knows when and if he ever needs me, I'm here for him. I had a couple of good years working with Joey, and then I never coached again. Not because of a lack of desire, but more because of a lack of time. Life is funny that way. I did some high school officiating for a few years and it kept me around the game but again, I had to walk away from it because of the time that it required on the weekends. My daughters were now living closer, just three hours away, and officiating was going to take too much time away from them and I wasn't willing to do that. It seemed as though my ties to the game I loved, the game that had always been a part of my DNA—football—were slowly fading away. All that remained were the opportunities to speak to kids who had aspirations of playing professional sports.

One time I spoke to a group of eighth grade boys in Philadelphia. There were about 20 of them and I asked them what they wanted to do when they grow up. All but one of them wanted to play in the NFL. That one kid wanted to own his own business, which elicited chuckles from all of the other kids. I then asked them if they knew the average career for an NFL player. I heard 15 years, no 12 years, no 20 years and so on. I just shook my head. I told them that the average career was a little over three years. In that moment, you could see nineteen jaws hit the floor. I then asked them what they would do for the rest of their lives after their three-year career was over. "No, really think about what you will do and tell me. I'll wait." They had no clue what else they wanted to do because the NFL was their sole aim. Then I pointed to the young man that wanted to own his own business and told them that he would probably make more money than all of them combined and that some of them may end up working for him. They all looked at him with a different set of eyes. I realized that was the story I needed to be sharing, and I set out to do just that.

I wanted to work with the NFL office and help current athletes and former athletes navigate the inevitable transition of their professional sports careers. I made a few visits to the NFL Players Association offices in Washington, DC and the NFL offices in New York. I'm a former player who has worked his butt off in the non-profit space; of course they could use my help. There were current players shooting themselves in the leg, committing suicide, getting busted for drug use and having various domestic violence issues. There were former players who were losing their money from making bad financial decisions and suffering from a lack of direction because they had no life plan established for their post careers. Of course, they would let me help, right? I guess I didn't know enough of the right people. I met with the people who could've made it happen but I guess I didn't have the right membership to the "political boys club." Damn shame too, because I really feel I could have added some value and helped these players. After all, I had been one of them and I had probably walked a similar path in one way, shape or form. Maybe it just wasn't meant be through the NFL, but I would figure out another way. That's the thing about an Underdog; we don't just give up at the first sign of adversity. If the door doesn't open for us initially, we create another door. I would find a way to have my voice heard and to help those who needed help, even if they didn't know they needed it. I was determined, and most importantly there were so many athletes out there who needed the knowledge and experience I had to share.

And then there are times when doors are created and opened, organically. I was asked to speak on a panel for the football team at my alma mater, the University of Virginia. It proved a turning point for me. While I may not have been able to work with current and former players of the NFL in an official capacity, I could mentor these college players. The panel discussion was very well received. In fact, they turned our discussions and comments into a recruiting video. Shortly thereafter, I was asked if I would be interested in interviewing for the radio Color Commentator position for the University's football team. The Lord moves stealthily and decisively. After interviewing, I was offered the opportunity and I happily accepted. I was once again around the game I loved, with an opportunity to mentor young men. The head coach was a tremendous leader of men and he and I had a relationship from years past. He, like me, was genuinely committed to player development off the field and outside of football. He would tell me about the issues some of the young men were going through and how there really seemed to be a void in their lives, or shall I say, a lack of an outlet for them to reach out to, other than him. He felt like they needed a person who they respected and who could give them guidance. He wanted a person that wasn't necessarily a coach or a parent. He allowed me to be around the guys to get to know them and to just fellowship with them. I got to know a lot of them and they respected me because they knew I could relate to their experience as student-athletes at an academically rigorous university. The more that I was around them, the more they could sense I cared about them. I began asking questions about their majors and how they planned to use their degree in their particular field of study. Frankly, I was disappointed with the answers I received. Most of them had no idea what they wanted to do if they didn't play in the NFL. I was floored, but then you only know what you're taught, right? I reached out to a former UVA alumnus, Dr. Angela Charlton, who worked out of the NFL office in New York transitioning players from the NFL into mainstream society by finishing college or getting into the workforce. I shared with her my observations and concerns regarding student-athletes, most recently those attending our alma mater, which only reinforced the importance of her work with the NFL. We began to put together a plan for teaching athletes life skills. We developed workshops to help open their eyes to their future, whether they played professional sports or not. The goal would be to teach them important skills to help them navigate themselves through life. My on- and off-field experiential knowledge and passion made me the ideal candidate to speak about it, to carry and deliver the message to targeted athletes. My colleague, in her role at the NFL, brought the clinical expertise. She had developed and managed all mandatory life skills and professional development player programs within the NFL. Additionally, she had earned a Master Degree in Counseling Education and Supervision and a Doctorate Degree in Counselor Education. We were a winning combination and we were so excited about the possibilities of the lives we could help. We put so much time into doing research and gathering information to design the workshops. We even developed pre- and post-test evaluations. It was a true labor of love. We were both invested because we knew there was a tremendous need for what we were offering. However, even the best laid plans are put on hold until God says it's the right time. He determines when the right lessons have been learned and challenges cleared. Many different obstacles blocked our path. Sometimes it was a job loss by one or both of us, or the call of day-to-day priorities and commitments. Several things caused our plans to be put on the back burner. One time we were actually, eleven days away from launching our first two workshops only to be told we would have to wait because priorities had changed and they wanted to make sure all parties were on the same page. We were devastated because we were so close to all of the fruits of our labor being realized. We were working with a coach who understood the importance of player development, and a representative of a Christian organization who was focused on athletes. The stars seemed to be aligning in our favor and then the door was slammed shut as we all attempted to walk through it. It felt like a punch in the stomach and I was disappointed beyond belief. I remember asking, "What is so wrong with wanting to help these athletes build a roadmap to a successful future?" A friend reminded me that God does things in His own time and that this was just a comma and not a period. It was hard to accept but I knew he was right. I had to put trust in God's plan. In that moment, I realized that God's plans supersede any good intentions I had and that I must make sure my plan is always in accordance with the plan He has for my life. As I reflect on my life on this journey of adversity and blessings, I now realize that when obstacles have blocked my path to success, that I have been working outside of God's plan. When things flow organically, then

I am right where He wants me to be. It took me over forty-eight years to arrive at this place of understanding, but it's better to have finally learned that life lesson so that it can be passed along than to spend a life not having a clue. I mean that's a part of my life mission—to serve—and I will work towards fulfilling that mission until He calls me home. The Underdog in me is always learning and is always growing spiritually. An Underdog understands the importance of faith. An Underdog will pull from the quote of Dr. Martin Luther King, Jr. who said, "Faith is taking the first step, even when you can't see the whole staircase."

Today, I continue to share my knowledge with some of the athletes who attend or have attended my alma mater. I owe it to them. I want to help them develop a plan for their lives. I want to teach them the importance of networking and having people in their corner, who can affect positive change in their lives. I want to impress upon them the importance of discovering their passion, something they love to do outside of sports. I want to show them the importance of making a difference in the lives of those who are less fortunate or in need of mentorship. We make a life by what we give and paying it forward is the very least we can do. A lot of these young men have dealt with adversity and worked their butts off to overcome it. I'm sure each one of them at one point or another had someone who stood in the gap and provided encouragement during those times of adversity. It is truly our duty to pay it forward.

ADVERSITY: Losing young lives, ripe with potential and talent, to the unfortunate pitfalls that plague too many of our nation's youth. BLESSINGS: Gaining the wisdom that I can use my life experiences to help shape, mold and save young lives.

# CHAPTER 8

## Man's Best Friend

I COULDN'T POSSIBLY share a part of my life without mentioning my love and affection for man's best friend, both of the four- and two-legged persuasion, that have been a part of my life. Those of you who really know me, know my love for dogs. In my adult life, I have had four of them. Starting in 1991, the roster went something like this: Que, the Boxer; Pearl, the Rottweiler; Tiger, the English Bulldog; and Hannibal, the Weimaraner. All had very different personalities, but all were extremely lovable. I would have to say Que was my favorite, because we were together for thirteen years and shared so many different experiences together. I remember the day I brought him home at 8 weeks old, and the day I laid him to rest thirteen years later. Que was my ace. We road tripped together and he bore witness to a lot of my life. He saw me as the young adult, still unknowingly dealing with the loss of my mother. He saw me as the dedicated athlete who refused to be outworked. He saw me wildin' out. He saw me struggle to find my way. He saw me become a husband and a father. Most importantly, he was always there with unconditional love. He was my child before I had children, my family, and my confidant. He showed me what loyalty was really about. My friends became his friends. We were two peas in a pod, if that's even possible. We went to the beach together and we even drank beer together.

When Pearl came into our lives during my second year in Tampa, Que showed her the ropes. The three of us had such great synergy. We were our own little family. Pearl was the big scary looking Rottweiler, who was also extremely lovable. I think of the days when the three of us would sit on the dock behind the house and look into the canal that led out to the bay. Just the three of us, in one big dog pile. A lot of those times I would just reflect on life and how much I missed my mom, wishing she were there. We had those dog piles often, though most of the time in front of the television. I remember Pearl barking at the manatees passing through the canal. I remember them both jumping through the screens of the lanai and running around barking when I had friends over in the swimming pool. One of the funniest sites was to look out of the window on a breezy day and see all of the screens blowing in the breeze. Que hung out in the house most of the time and Pearl favored the garage. I remember being out of town for a few days one time, and returning home before picking up the dogs from the kennel. I pulled into the garage and as I approached the kitchen door it felt like I was walking through a thick spider web. The garage had literally become a flea market. I had on a pair of white socks and they almost turned black from being covered with fleas. I got eaten alive that day and every day until I got those suckers out of the garage. I eventually decided to breed Pearl. She had several puppies and she stayed with a family I trusted until most of the pups were sold or given away. I eventually gave Pearl to that family. She was happy there with her pups and the family had young kids who could give Pearl more quality time when she needed it. I was doing a lot of traveling during football season with games every week, so when the family asked if she could stay with them for good, I let her go with them. It was hard to break up our little family, but Pearl needed the attention she received from that family and I wanted her to be happy and healthy. So, it was just Que and I again, at least for a little while.

When I signed with the Seattle Seahawks I was away for the season in Seattle and Que was back in Tampa staying at the house with my friend from college, Terry. While in Seattle, I visited a breeder of Neapolitan Mastiffs and English Bulldogs right outside of Canada. I purchased a purebred English bulldog. He was an all-white, slobbery marshmallow that I fell in love with immediately and named him Tiger. When the season was over, Tiger went to Philly with my then girlfriend, Leslie, and I returned to Tampa. Tiger and Que would finally meet after about a year and they hit it off like old friends. Tiger was a bit high maintenance with several required eye surgeries, but he was truly a lovable dog. He was perfectly content to sleep all day and his top speed was slow motion. It was always a slow pace with him and that suited Que just fine, as he was getting a little long in the tooth and slowing down. They entertained each other and they entertained Leslie and me. Then I decided to purchase a Weimaraner. I really got the idea when I met the actress, Salli Richardson's, dogs while on a trip to LA for a golf tournament. She was playing in the tournament and invited a few of us over for dinner. Her Weimaraners were awesome. They were lovable, loyal and laid back. I decided to get one myself and I named him Hannibal. Such a cool name, I thought. Hannibal was beautiful. He was just a pup when I brought him home, but he was long and lean with the most incredible grey eyes. As I mentioned earlier, Que was getting a little older, but he still had spurts when he was as hyper as he had been always been. Once Hannibal entered the house, it was as if Que was reborn. It was like Hannibal became the fountain of youth for Que. Hannibal grew into this muscular amazing specimen and Que was right there letting him know that he was the four-legged Alpha male dog of the household. Tiger displayed bursts of energy and the three of them would wrestle and pin each other down, take a water break, and then go it again. It was awesome to see Que back to a semblance of his old self. Right around the same time that Que started really slowing down, my first daughter, Kennedy, was born. All three dogs were great with her and very patient and protective. It was if they all knew she was a fragile baby and they were her big bothers and guardians. It was amazing to see.

Que's health started going downhill fast, because he was getting old. He struggled to stand most days and I had to start carrying him outside to use the bathroom. His veterinarian told me that it was only a matter of time before I would have to make some tough decisions. It pained me to see him suffering, but it was hard to let him go. I eventually took him back to his vet to end his suffering. As he and I laid there on the floor, he rested his head on my leg and looked up at me with those big brown eyes as if to say, "You and I have had a good ride old friend, but it's time to let me go. Your mom will look after me now and I need you to go take care of that little girl of yours." As the doctor gave him the injection that would give him eternal sleep, I watched his eyes close for the last time. I was heartbroken. His vet and all the staff were crushed as well, as they had treated him and gotten to know him as long I as I had him. I cried all of the way home. It's been 14 years since he's been gone and my eyes still fill up with tears as I write this, as if I'm right back in that moment. That night, as I walked into the house with bloodshot eyes still filled with tears, the first face I saw was Kennedy's. She looked up at me and started smiling. In the midst of my tears and heartache, that smile soothed my heartache. I picked her up and hugged her tight. Que was put into my life for a reason. There were things I was supposed to learn from him. His final look at me in the vet's office said everything. "Let me go," and "I need you to take care of that little girl." Only God could have put those words in my heart, at that time, at that place, in Que's last moments with me.

Now when I referenced the two-legged version of man's best friend, I was referring to the members of the greatest brotherhood on the planet. The brothers of Omega Psi Phi Fraternity, Inc., affectionately known as "Que Dogs" or "the Bruhs," have been integral in my life. My line brothers, Dele, Earl, Darwin, Stafford and Dave, started a journey with me over twenty-six years ago creating a lifetime bond. We were six different personalities that become one coming out of the darkness of our own self-centered lives and into the light of Omega. We faced the fiery crucible and crossed the burning sands together. It was one of the most difficult things I have ever done in life and I am forever thankful and blessed to have gone through it with these five guys. We have all grown up, and while most of us have kids and careers today, we never forget about each other. While we all don't get to see each other often, it is always extremely special when we do. The bond is what makes it special and it will forever unite us. When we do get together, we talk about our pledge process and the many things we went through together. We talk about our families and those brothers who we may have lost since the last time we saw each other. There is nothing like the Bruhs. There are too many to mention, but I will shout out a few of them.

Once again, I believe God has always strategically placed Bruhs into my life. There have been Bruhs who have been there for guidance and instruction: Kevin Best, Tony Freeman, Doug Jackson and Rodney Hopson stand out in that regard. Bruhs who could open doors through their multitude of connections: Marvin Dickerson, Gary Flowers and Darrel German immediately pop into my head. Steve Ivory, affectionately known as "Bam," taught me a lot about being a Bruh. He pledged at Virginia State University and I'm blessed that he was born and raised in Charlottesville, VA, where the University of Virginia is located. He was an integral part of my pledge process. He took me under his wing and welcomed me into his home. He is one of the most important Bruhs in my life. In fact, our bond has always been greater than fraternal. We have been family for a long time. There were times when I would stop by his house just to visit his mom. She was an incredible person with a big personality and a unique way of showing you she cared. If you knew Momma Ivory, then you knew she gave it to you straight up, no chaser. Her son, Steve, is the same. He showed me so many things about being a good Bruh. He passed on knowledge and he taught me how to road trip. He taught me that the power in the brotherhood is the singular moments when you and a brother can just sit and share your bond. He and I have shared so many great times together, but the ones that stand out the most are the times when he and I are just sitting across the table from each other sipping on Crown Royal, talking for hours. We still do it to this day. We also share the bond of losing our moms. Bam was there for me when I lost my mother and I was there for him when his mom passed away. It was important to be there for him then and always because he has always been there for me.

Then there is Elijah Alexander. He pledged at Kansas State and was drafted by the Tampa Bay Buccaneers when I was playing with them. He was another Bruh that just touched your soul if you had the pleasure to meet him. We bonded immediately when he first arrived in Tampa. We were truly kindred spirits and we did a lot together. We had a ritual of grilling out every week and just chilling. Once again it was that brother-to-brother bonding that Bam talked about that made our time together special. It was always an unselfish willingness to be there for one another just because you wanted to be there. It was unspoken but it was understood. I remember when he met his future wife, Kim. There was just something unique about her that stood out to me. She had a kind spirit and she was just so genuine. I think she could see through our craziness and could recognize the incredible man within Elijah. They would eventually marry each other and start a family together. Elijah and I lost touch through the years. I left Tampa because of free agency and headed to Seattle while he eventually headed to play for the Oakland Raiders. I discovered many years later that he had been battling a form of cancer called Multiple Myeloma, which is the number one blood cancer affecting African Americans. We caught up with each other many years after our playing days when he came to Washington, DC as an advocate in the fight against Multiple Myeloma. We hadn't seen each other in years, so it was great to catch up and talk over dinner. I remember being so happy to see him. We talked as if we hadn't missed a day of each other's lives. I told him that we had to do better at staying in touch and trying to see each other. We agreed to do so, but we never got that opportunity. He passed away two years later. Our bond could not be broken by the years of absence from one another, nor by the distance that separated us, and not even by death. He is in the Omega Chapter now, the chapter to which all brothers who have departed this earthly world belong, but I feel him in my heart and I know he's got some ribs on the grill and is setting out a hop as he looks down on us from above.

Abdul Hoggard, I referenced him in an earlier chapter, is the closest thing to an "old skool" Bruh that I have ever met. He pledged at Elizabeth City State University and I met him through my chapter Bruh, Tony Freeman. We hit it off immediately. We pledged nine years apart and hadn't known each other for very long, but connected like we had known each other for many, many years. I firmly believe that you learn what a man is made of when you hear his journey. Our fraternal bond was made stronger by sharing our life experiences with each other. There were stories of time growing up in the country in North Carolina and the hardships associated with that. There were shared stories of achieving the pinnacle of financial success and then finding the valleys of total financial ruin. There were shared stories of relationships, marriage and divorce. We met at a time when he didn't really know a lot of people in the DC area. Initially, I think I served as an outlet for him, instead of sitting home being bored, but he became an integral part of my life. We traveled and played golf together. When we first started playing golf, he was terrible. I talked so much trash and beat the brakes off of him so many times. We would play a little 9-hole course at the Soldiers Home with Billy Strudwick, another one of my chapter brothers, and we would make little one dollar bets here and there. I had a little plastic cup in the back of my truck and I had written Abdul's name on the cup with a blue piece of tape. I called it my Abdul donation cup. It got to a point where I was giving him strokes and then he didn't want the strokes anymore. Part of that was because of ego, but it was the only way he could at least have a chance. I told him that I was a firm believer in continuing to whip his butt until he got tired of losing and practiced until he could stop me from winning. Him beating me would take a couple of years, because even though his game improved incredibly, he was so focused on beating me that he still couldn't get over the mental hump of the game. I told him that he couldn't beat me because he was too busy playing against me rather than playing against the golf course. Once he started doing that, he would beat me every once in a while. It probably would have happened more often if I weren't such a Jedi Master. He has an incredible mind for information technology, and he would have me cracking up at the stories of when he used to be a hacker and ended up getting caught, but eventually working for the government. I would listen to him talk about the work he had done installing systems for organizations, and eventually establishing his own consulting firm. My dude is an IT wizard, but don't get it twisted. If the two of us had to walk down a dark alley and some guys rolled up on us, he would stand there with me, back to back, ready for battle, if necessary. I know without a doubt that I can always count on him. We are both hardwired to be loyal to a fault. I also learned that the hardships he has battled through in life have primarily been endured alone. He is a prideful brother and too damn stubborn to ask for help. I remember saying to him that pride is like a beard that must be trimmed daily. I could relate though, because I have been that way for a majority of my life. Although there have been many times in my adult life when I have felt that I had to count on me so I wouldn't have to worry about someone else disappointing me. It took growth for me to unlearn that line of thinking. I've had to look to my past and remember some of the lessons my mother taught me. People will disappoint you regardless. Control what can be controlled and keep your circle of close friends to a minimum. One thing that I have always had to emphasize to him is that those days of enduring challenges alone are over because he is a part of *my* circle. I showed him, through my actions that I am in his life and my duty is to always serve my brother. I let him know that I would never leave him nor forsake him just as God would never do that to any of His children. He still struggles with that, but either he is getting better at realizing I'm here to help if he needs me or I'm getting better at interjecting my hand of help when I think he needs it. But to be clear, most of the help I provide is through words of wisdom and encouragement. He does the same thing for me and he has a gift of knowing just when it's needed. It's funny because we both seem to know when each other needs that encouraging shot in the arm or that motivating foot in the butt. I would go to the mat for this dude anytime, anywhere. He is just a great dude and I would trust him with my life. I don't say that often so he is in rarefied air. That is the kind of bond that can only be shared by men who have gained insight from their personal experiences and have spent time together developing that bond. We should all be so lucky to have a lifetime bond in our fellow man. I can't imagine the last twenty-seven years of my life without my fraternity brothers, and if I'm blessed to see another twenty-seven years with the frat, then it will have been a good life. Friendship is essential to my soul and I am eternally grateful that God has blessed me with that gift. My dogs provided a consistent love and companionship that was critical and arrived exactly when I needed it. The Bruhs gave me a brotherhood and friendship beyond my wildest dreams. There is something very important about men coming together to teach each other to become good men, good fathers and good citizens. My fraternity brothers have provided me a safe haven to be vulnerable without being judged, but have also held my feet to the fire when it comes to accountability. As black men, we all need to come together and fight for the things that are most important to us instead of possessing a "crabs in a barrel" mentality that only divides us. Whether you have grown up with a father or not, we owe it to each other to uplift one another and lift as we climb.

ADVERSITY: Losing some of man's best friends.
BLESSINGS: Finding fraternal bonds that can never be broken, even in death.

# CHAPTER 9

## Moments of Clarity and Reflection

WOW... AS I look back over the past forty plus years, there are so many things that I have learned and there are so many things for which I am thankful. What follows are the moments of clarity and reflection that have helped me shape, what I hope to be, a better version of myself. While I don't know your journey, I hope you are able to take away some nugget of insight that provides you clarity, inspiration or motivation to keep on keeping on. To keep standing up, never defeated, like a tenacious Underdog. I pray you will remember to love yourself first, and then observe and learn from the lessons all around us...in everything.

1. *There is life in every breath.* This is one of the biggest things that I have learned. It seems so simple but we miss out on that little carrot every single day. Every breath you take is a gift from God, so don't waste it and be thankful for every breath you take. Value each breath and leave your mark in every one.

2. *Don't ever give away your joy.* I don't really like the popular phrase; don't let anyone take away your joy, because no one can take away what is God-given. No one can take away His gift. Joy can only be given away so why would you ever give away a gift that God has given you?

3. *When I was a child, I talked like a child, I thought like a child, I reasoned like a child. When I became a man, I set aside*

*those childish ways.* (1 Corinthians 13:11) Sometimes it is hard to be a grown-up, but grow up we must. Let us learn the lessons of our youth so that we can make this world a better place as adults. I know it may sound cliché, but I'm determined to do just that. By learning from our childish ways, we can help develop a better generation of children, who currently have way too much access to the world. As grown-ups, we must help to govern that access and help our children to create their own narrative.

4.  *Parents must be present in the lives of their children.* We live in different times and this same access to a bigger, more globalized world will be the death of future generations if we are not active in their lives. They deal with a different set of issues than we had to deal with growing up, but that doesn't mean that we can quit on them. I'll take my chances with being the parent who has challenging kids who I'm willing to fight with and fight for, then the parent who will trust society to teach them what it means to be a grown up. Fathers must play a better role. They must teach their sons how to become men, whether they grew up with a father or not. If you don't know how to be a father, ask for help from the positive men in your life. If you don't have one, then call me. Enough is enough. Fathers of daughters, be present, even when you can't be there physically every day. My daughters live in another state, but I call them every day. I know they may not want to speak with me every day, but I need to hear their voices to make sure that they are "good" and because it gives me strength. And they need to hear my voice as a constant provider of authentic concern, interest, support and direction in their lives. They know beyond any doubt I am here for them, for anything. I know there

may be challenges, but as a man aren't you up for any challenge involving your daughter? You are the example she will look to when it comes time for her to choose her mate. Make sure you give her an example that would make your mother proud. Your children will walk in your footsteps if you leave them good ones to follow. Be present to help design the blueprint for your children's lives. Introduce them to God and let them know that even when you aren't there God is always with them. They can trust God's path because He is the way, the truth and the life. And if they stray from the path, be present enough to help steer them back on it.

5. *"And if you leave God's path and go astray, you will hear a Voice behind you say, No, this is the way; walk here."* (Isaiah 30:21) I have failed so many times, but I have succeeded so much more. I have left that path more times than I care to mention, and God has accepted me back each time. God and I can be walking along His path and life is just great and out of nowhere I hear the world calling. It always seems like the world is having so much fun and each and every time I remove my hand from His and deviate from the path, He is there, patiently waiting to save me. He pulls the thorns out of my butt and watches as I dust myself off. I sheepishly look at Him as He extends His hand for us to continue forward. He could have left me there and continued on without me, but He didn't and He won't because He said that He wouldn't. When you have a relationship with Him, you gain that understanding that He promised to never leave us nor forsake us. None of us is perfect and when we fall we know we can get back up again. Those who don't have a relationship with Him are quick to fall into a "woe is

me" type of space. They don't realize that they are never alone because they don't realize the price has been paid for their sins. The cost was more than any of us deserve but the Master loves us, in spite of ourselves. I'm not trying to preach a sermon but when I reflect on the sacrifice that was given for me, it brings me to my knees. I'm humbled because He gave up His only son for us all. Would you be willing to sacrifice your child for a thankless and selfish people? It really puts things into perspective for me.

6. *Live in the moment.* Life is precious and each day is not promised, so live each day more abundantly. I have lost people in my life and it has made no sense to me whatsoever. I have had friends taken down by illness like a thief in the night, and have been left saying "I should have" or "I was going to spend time." It's so easy to think that we will always have time but you never really know when your number will be called. Hug your children, kiss your significant other, and tell your parents you love them. They could be gone in the next instance so by all means, live in the moment.

7. *Friendship is essential to the soul.* The true essence of friendship is being present. It's not the deeds or the words but it's the presence. It's time spent just being. Whether it's being a sounding board, a safe place to swim to in a storm, a voice of reason or whatever the case may be. Just be present. They say people are put into your life for a reason, a season or a lifetime. When you're present in your friendships, you will see which category each friend falls into and you'll be a better friend as a result of that.

8. *If the people you have in your life don't enhance it, get rid of them.* They are just taking up space and life is too short for

space-eaters. Pray about the people who come into your life and ask God why they are there. Ask Him to remove the ones who are only dream-takers and do nothing to fill your bucket. Life is a series of givers and takers. If you have more takers in your life than you have givers, you have some spring cleaning to do. It's not personal but you should view space in your life as valuable, and if people can't add value, they can only diminish the return. Nobody has time for that. My old boss used to tell me he didn't really like people and that everyone started out on his "don't like you" list and it was up to them to work their way off of it. I always thought that was one heck of a weeding out process. People who are concerned about you and are there to enhance your life will work their way off of that list organically. It won't be a heavy lift for them. Those who never make it off of the list weren't ever going to bring value to your life anyway, and they should remain on the list by their actions or lack thereof. As I stated earlier, I have learned to ask God if the people who are coming into my life are brought by Him. If they are not, then please redirect them away from me.

9.  *Love is patient and love is kind so never take love for granted.* If we had more love in the world it would be a better place. If someone loves you and you don't love them back, it's better to tell them that you care for them but not in that way. It may hurt initially but they will respect your honesty later. Unfortunately, heartbreak is a part of life and we all have to deal with it at some point. But to quote Jalil from the great rap group, Whodini, "I guess it's better to have loved and to have lost than to never have loved at all." Heartbreak either teaches us how to love better or it makes us afraid to love again. No one wants to feel the pain of

that heartbreak ever again. We must be careful not to allow that fear t of heartbreak stunt our loves ability to grow. By shielding ourselves from heartbreak we are shielding ourselves from love and are only depriving the object of our affection. One truism is that if you are going to open yourself up to love someone fully and with all of you, then unfortunately you will have to allow the possibility of being hurt to enter too. There is no one-sided coin here. Love fully, love hard and let the chips fall where they may. Love fearlessly because there is no fear in love. Perfect love drives out fear. Remember God's love is at the core of who we are. Romans 8:38-39 states, "Neither death nor life, neither angels nor demons, neither the present nor the future, nor any powers, neither height nor depth, nor anything else in all creation, will be able to separate us from the love of God that is in Christ Jesus our Lord."

10. *To thine own self be true.* This is my lifetime mantra. Never, ever stray away from who you really are at your core. You have to be cool with the person you see in the mirror each day. It's alright to emulate or to imitate, if that's your thing, but don't get caught up trying to live someone else's life. Create your own path and leave your mark. Create footsteps for others to follow. Be the absolute best at whatever you strive to do in life, but make it mean something to you.

11. *We make a life by what we give.* All the money in the world won't make you happy. Make your life one of service. Give back to those who are less fortunate, either financially or by giving of your time. I've dedicated my life to service and while I'll probably never be financially rich, I am rich beyond measure because of the lives I have helped to change through that service. My mother was a giver and I am

my mother's child. I have always been about vehicles for change in helping others. A characteristic of an Underdog is a willingness to give to others and to help those in need An Underdog will also fight for those who may not have been dealt a fair hand in life, but who find a way to keep on fighting. I will always be a champion for them and I wouldn't bet against me if I were you.

12. *Find a career, not just a job.* Find something you are passionate about and make that your career. They say if you love what you do you will never work a day in your life. It won't always be easy, but it will be worth it. If someone would've told me that I would have been doing non-profit work for over sixteen years, I would have never believed them, but I'm passionate about it. The path was revealed to me later in life, so be patient with yourself in discovering your passion. Open your mind to possibilities, to dreams, and your passion will follow.

13. *God has me exactly where He wants me right now.* It's not really about what I want right now because I believe He is preparing me for something great. "For I know the plans that I have for you," says the Lord. They are plans for good and not disaster, to give you a future and a hope. In those days when you pray, I will listen." (Jeremiah 29:11-12) I am just a chess piece on His chess board and He is the chess master. The difficult part is that I am human and I want what I want when I want it. I'm also smart enough to realize He does things in His time and He tells us when we are ready, not the other way around. Is it a test of patience? Absolutely! I have also failed so many times trying to force my own path without realizing the path I want may not be the path

He has for me. I have had to learn that He manipulates the chess board and I move when He moves me. I still work on the side hustle strategy but I am cognizant that when doors begin to open up organically it is Him guiding the ship. When momentum slows down or obstacles start to appear, I fall back because that's my sign that He is telling me to put it on the back burner for a minute. It took some growth to get to that point. I am a work in progress and I'm forever growing in my walk with Him. I am not perfect and, yes, I am flawed, but I am His.

14. Rudyard Kipling stated in his poem, IF, *if you can wait and not be tired by waiting, or being lied about, don't deal in lies; Or being hated, don't deal in hating, and yet don't look too good nor talk too wise."* Don't give way to hating or being lied about; don't deal in lies." People will lie and hate on you because they are mad they aren't you. They are mad that you are willing to do what they wouldn't. They are mad that you are willing to put yourself through the process required for greatness and that they just don't have it in them. They rejoice in your failure and they *talk* about what they're going to do instead of just doing it. H.A.T.E.R.S really are **H**umbled **A**t **T**he **E**ventual **R**esounding **S**uccess. *Your* resounding success. Let that marinate for a minute.

15. *Create your own definition of success.* Success can mean different things to different people. Control your own narrative on what success really looks like to you, then go take success…it's yours.

16. *"Endure hardness as a good soldier for Christ."* (2 Timothy 2:3) No one ever said life would be easy, but you get out of

it what you put into it.  If it gives you lemons, then make the best damn lemonade imaginable.

17.  *NO EXCUSES.* Excuses build bridges to nowhere and those who use them will amount to nothing.  Excuses are just self-imposed obstacles.  Excuses < GREATNESS.

18.  *There is nothing worse than wasted potential.*  If you have the potential to be great, then be great.  If you have the potential to change the world, then change the world.  Never be fearful of tapping into your potential to be great.  Potential is that place between process and greatness.  Love the PROCESS, tap into your POTENTIAL, and GREATNESS will follow.

19.  *Control what you can control.*  Trying to do anything else leads to nothing but angst and frustration.  I can't tell you how many times I have been so angry about things that were not in my power to control.  Incidentally, that is a byproduct of caring about a particular thing and having a passion for it.  That isn't necessarily a bad thing, as long as you can manage your frustration.  If you didn't care or have a passion for things, then they wouldn't frustrate you.

20.  *"Who of you by worrying can add a single hour to your life? Since you cannot do this very little thing, why do you worry about the rest?"* (Luke 12:25-26) God told us in the Bible, not to worry about tomorrow because tomorrow will worry about itself.  Besides, worry is too heavy a burden to carry around.  Our shoulders were not designed to carry burdens that God was meant to carry.  Don't worry, He's got it! Reminds me of graffiti I saw painted on a fence in Oregon that read, "Worry is a misuse of imagination." That gem was a drop the mic moment.

21. *Don't slap away the hand of grace just because it doesn't look the way you thought it would.* I once prayed for a better job and God answered my prayer. Because it was in another state, away from my church home and friends, I questioned if it was the right thing to do. My pastor said, "Your children are there so what else is there to discuss." God had provided grace but I didn't recognize His grace because it didn't look the way I thought it would. It works out like that sometimes, so be on the lookout for unrecognizable grace and when you realize it, give Him all the praise for it.

22. *"Without faith, it is impossible to please God."* (Hebrews 11:6) I heard a pastor say that the Bible is the basic instruction before leaving Earth. He also said there is a direct connection between faith and power. More faith creates more power for you to possess, which translates into you having more blessings. Faith truly connects our weakness to God's strength. So, let's get strong.

23. *Growth requires change.* Unfortunately, that change sometimes comes with fear of loss. Sometimes that loss is accompanied by pain. Don't let fear of loss or fear of pain stunt your growth. Fear is a mind-killer and if you want to realize the change that growth requires, you have to be willing to put yourself to the hazard. GROWTH > FEAR.

24. *Find your non-negotiable.* Find that one thing that you are passionate about, that makes you feel whole, that restores you. For me, it used to be running because that was my release and the time that I felt like God was talking to me and I was actually receiving His Word. Believe it or not, golf has become my non-negotiable. That may make me a glutton for punishment but golf does it for me. God still talks to me

on the course but our conversations are little different. Golf is the most challenging sport that I have ever played and it somehow recharges my battery. It's akin to finding my beach!

25. *Together Excellence Always Materializes,* my acronym for T.E.A.M. The power of a team mentality is great. Whether it's sports or in the corporate space, the team concept is valuable when it comes to overall success. It gives people the opportunity to work together towards a common goal and then share in the ownership and success of attaining that goal. Individual success is cool, but it can't hold a candle to the success of a T.E.A.M.

26. *Sometimes you can't go around it. Sometimes the only path is to go through it.* "Black may be the clouds about you and your future may seem grim, but don't let your nerve desert you; keep yourself in fighting trim. If the worst is bound to happen, spite of all that you can do, running from it will not save you, SEE IT THROUGH!"-Edgar A. Guest

27. *Don't let your ego impede your progress. It ain't always about you.* Many a man or woman has faltered by being in their own way. They blocked their blessing because they were too stubborn and egotistical to realize they were the problem. There is a fine line between ego, arrogance and confidence. It is great to have confidence and to have belief in self, but it is foolish to think that it's all about you. Individual abilities are all gifts from God and we had nothing to do with it. Ego says, "I'm responsible for my greatness and I owe my success to no one but myself." Tragic words of a loser. "For by the grace given me I say to every one of you: Do not think of yourself more highly than you ought, but rather think of yourself with sober judgment, in

accordance with the faith God has distributed to each of you." (Romans 12:3) In all things, give Him the glory.

28. *Happiness is a choice.* If you choose to be happy then you will be happy. Your happiness is not dependent upon someone else, your current situation or circumstance. Your happiness starts with you. If you're feeling unhappy, then just take the time to look at your blessings and then look at someone who is less fortunate. Things could always be worse, so count your blessings and thank God for every gift He has given you.

29. *Every superhero should have a side hustle.* I've been saying this for years. If you're living check to check or you want your financial situation to improve, then take an inventory of the talent that you possess and create a strategy to improve your finances. Most people do not love the work they do, but understand the bills have to be paid. We toil in these jobs just surviving, instead of really living. Life is too short just to be surviving. I have found my passion and it has taken me a while to put the pieces in place, but I am moving forward. Part of the hesitation has been fear of failure, but then I realized if I changed just one life it all was worth it. I also had the counsel of friends who assured me I was on the right path and that I should just take those things I have been keeping on the back burner and move them to the front burner. Will it be easy to manage everything all at once? No, but it will be worth it in the end. The life of a superhero is never easy, but they manage to figure it all out and that's what makes them super.

30. *The grass isn't always greener on the other side. It's only green where you decide to water it.* If you put a concerted

and genuine effort into the things that really matter to you, they will prosper. Once again, you get out of it what you put in to it.

31. *Terror must be maintained or the empire will crumble.* I'm going to leave that one right there. Those who are "in the know" will know exactly what that means.

32. *One of the hardest and easiest things to do is to have for- giveness.* When someone has hurt us deeply the natural tendency is to retaliate. In those times, we have to remem- ber God forgave us so we must also forgive others who have wounded us. "Do not do wrong to repay a wrong, and do not insult to repay an insult. But repay with a blessing, because you yourselves were called to do this so that you might receive a blessing." (1 Peter 3:9) I know this is easier said than done, but as my Uncle Donny told me, "Your sinful nature died on the cross, your human nature did not!" Let that marinate for a minute.

33. *Criticism is a part of life. Deal with it.* The great part about being an Underdog is proving people wrong and outlast- ing your critics. A lot stems from the fear of rejection. It forces people to hang on to things that are not to their benefit. It forces them to listen to the masses and to go outside of themselves in the hope of gaining acceptance. People get so worried and worked up about the judgment and opinions of others. What you eat doesn't make them go to the bathroom. Taking constructive criticism is one thing because it is for your betterment, but any other criti- cism or judgment that denigrates you needs to roll right off your back. Remember, you don't live to please man. You live to please God and ONLY GOD CAN JUDGE YOU! "In

view of all this, what can we say? If God is for us, who can be against us?" (Romans 8:31)

34. *Seeing a therapist can be, well... therapeutic.* I know they say black men don't go to the doctor or they don't do therapy. BREAKING NEWS: That is a closed-minded way of thinking and I can say it has helped me tremendously in the past. As men, we don't discuss what's going on with us internally. We bottle it up or compartmentalize it while keeping the grind steady. We don't realize we are doing more harm than good, and we are leading ourselves down a potential path of self-destruction. We become frustrated and our very essence begins to deteriorate. Our overall physical and mental health are impacted and that affects our work, our marriages and our families. And sadly, we don't even realize it because no one ever told us. Fella's, do yourself a favor and don't let pride get in the way of saving your life. It's okay to slow the grind down to 30 mph. Get your physical and mental health on point and recharge your batteries. Remember, the world will not stop and life is too damn short. Also, never forget, "these mountains that you are carrying, you were only supposed to climb." (Najwa Zebian)

35. *I never lose. Either I win or I learn.* (Nelson Mandela) That is the new mantra for Underdog moving forward. Nine words with tremendous impact that will now be the starting point for whatever I attempt. Greatness comes with either winning or learning.

# CHAPTER 10

## For My Daughters

I WANT TO leave this world a better place for my daughters, Kennedy and Carter. I want to share with them some of the valuable lessons I have learned over my lifetime in the hope that they won't make some of the same mistakes I have made. I know they will make their share of mistakes, but I pray I am there to catch them when they fall. I also must have the understanding that I have to let them fall and scrape their knee sometimes, because if they don't they will never gain the knowledge that they have the ability to heal and overcome. As a parent, we always want the best for our children and we always want to surround them with the best examples of good people, because it truly does take a village. They don't have the luxury of knowing the strength of their great grandmother, Viola Hairston. They weren't privileged to know the strength, courage and caring of my mother and their grandmother, Princetta. However, they do have two women in their lives who are pillars of strength, in their mother, Leslie, and my wife, Ericka. I had a conversation with Kennedy one day about both of them. I told her the stories of what both women have had to endure and how their strength and faith in God carried them through some very difficult times. We talked candidly about her mother's battle with breast cancer and about our failed marriage. There is no doubt her mother is a fighter. I then told her about Ericka's strength. How she worked multiple jobs to fund her college education, for which she has attained a bachelor's, a master's and a doctorate degree. She did this while being a single mom of two boys, raising them on her own with virtually no support. Many times I have seen her cry, not as a sign of weakness, but as a sign of fatigue and release, in preparation for the next challenge that was sure to come her way. Her sons will never know the sacrifices she had to make for them, but that's what parents do. I told her that I want to do my best to make Ericka's life better and provide her with the things she truly deserves. She is an extension of me, and while she would never try to replace their mother, she loves them and will be there for them. While they never got to meet their great grandmother and grandmother to bear witness to their strength, I see that same strength in my daughters. They both have been wonderfully and beautifully made by God, and they have a village whose role it is to help them get through this beautiful thing called life. We will provide guidance, discipline and love, the most important being love. They both will face adversity in their lives at some point but my hope is that they will learn along the way that adversity is a part of life and that what doesn't kill them will definitely make them stronger. It is our role as a village to teach them that too. We have to teach them that it's not how you start the race of life, it's how you finish it. Life is a marathon and not a sprint. Our instruction must be inclusive of an understanding that blessings are birthed through adversity and to not get too high with the victories or too low with the defeats. Life is a series of tests and that you have to pass the test in order to get to the next one. If you fail the test, then you repeat the test. There are lessons in failures if they don't allow the defeats to knock them off center too much. The village must teach them that there will be more victories than there will be defeats, and to never acknowledge that they lost but that they either won or they learned. We will teach them to always believe in themselves because if they don't believe in themselves then how can they ever expect others to believe in them. I pray that they will learn to be confident, respectful and humble. Confidence comes from a belief in self and humility keeps it from becoming arrogance. I hope my daughters will be better than I ever was. I hope they will realize that every blessing that comes their way is a rainbow after a storm and they should give thanks for every single rainbow. I hope they realize they will never have to want for love because I love them more than life itself. They are the best of all that I am and I thank God, every day for giving me the two best gifts imaginable.

# *Conclusion*

WHEN I STARTED this project, I didn't know how it would turn out. I questioned whether anyone would want to read a book about a guy who played in the NFL for few years and wasn't a superstar. The jury is still out on that, but this process has been very cathartic for me. I shed some tears while writing this, both from expected painful memories and uncovering feelings that still unknowingly haunt me. I guess when you've spent a lot of your younger years compartmentalizing and suppressing things to manage pain instead of really dealing with them, they will eventually rise to the surface in one way or another. By sharing a portion of my life, I have healed some damaged areas deep down inside, so this project was worth it. My hope was always that by showing a little insight into my life and my willingness to fight through adversity, that someone would see that if I could do it then they could do it too. I don't know what's going on in your life right now, but I want to assure you that you are not alone. No matter what your circumstances are currently, just know you can overcome anything with a willingness to work your tail off and by beginning to trust in God more than you ever have before.

I am a witness that prayer changes things. In my darkest hours, I had nowhere to look but to God, and that is the only place I needed to look. I gained strength that I didn't know I possessed and a confidence that I could overcome anything with God at my side. I am far from perfect, but He knows my heart is genuine and that I am real to my core. God showed me that I wasn't going through those tough times alone because we all face them. He showed me during those tough times that your response to challenge is what builds character and that character will guide you to your destiny. It reminds me of a scene from the movie The Last Samurai when Katsumoto (Ken Watanabe) and Captain Algren (Tom Cruise) were about to stage their final battle. Katsumoto asked Captain Algren, "You believe a man can change his destiny?" Algren responded, "I think a man does what he can, until his destiny is revealed." That line has stuck with me because it holds so much damn truth. We all have a journey to take and a path to walk. I've learned that my path is already chosen for me and that it really is up to me to trust in the path and trust in the plan until my destiny is revealed. It took some spiritual growth to get to that point and I am still working through it because I get anxious sometimes. God has a way of sending me gentle reminders that He's got it and to just trust in Him. My final few thoughts are that adversity really is about perspective. It can cripple you if you let it. It can consume you and drive you to a deep dark place if you give it the power to do so. Blessings are to show us that there is a light at the end of that tunnel of adversity. They are created to bring us closer to God because we cannot create blessings on our own. They are gifts that can only be given by God. Three things that adversity has taught me are: 1. Patience, 2. Humility, and 3. Trust in God.

1.  *Patience* is difficult because I want what I want and I want it when I want it. I think it's just human nature rearing its head repeatedly. The realization that God does things in His own time is something we all have to grow into accepting. Some

of us are a little more hardheaded than others, so the lesson hits a little harder. "Rejoice in hope, be patient in tribulation, be constant in prayer." (Romans 12:12)

2. *Humility* is about having that balance between confidence and arrogance while giving praise to another. Translation, I spent a lifetime believing in myself. I gained confidence in myself each time I overcame obstacles creating more confidence. Success followed as well as a belief that I can accomplish anything once I set my mind and focus on a goal. Then I had setbacks that forced me to realize it wasn't about me. At my worst, there came the realization that my life was about being a servant for my God and giving Him the glory through my successes. I realized that I'm not that special and that everything I have is a result of His gifts I was blessed to receive. Sure, I worked my tail off for everything I've achieved, but He provided the talent, the will and the ability. He sculpted me into what He wanted me to be and trusted me to be a good steward of His creation. When I went outside of what He wanted, then He provided corrective measures. It is about His plan, His time, and for His glory. These realizations only come with growth. "He leads the humble in what is right, and teaches the humble His way." (Psalms 25:9)

3. *Trust in God* is also a growth measure. "Trust in the Lord with all your heart and do not lean on your own understanding. In all your ways acknowledge Him, and He will make straight your paths." (Proverbs 3:5-6) Trusting in the plan He has laid out for my life has been a struggle because of that patience thing that I discussed earlier. I've struggled with feeling I have had to be all things for all

people. I've been that rock for others to swim to in a storm and cling to for protection. It has always been a role that I was more than happy to fill for others. But I often asked myself, "What happens when the rock needs?" I had to learn that God is the rock that I need to cling to for security and I had to trust in that. It was not easy to do that and I will humbly admit that I am still a work in progress. The weight of carrying around worry, burden and stress were just too damn heavy. That feeling of carrying around the weight of the world on your shoulders was Tony Covington personified. Through my adversity came the realization that man is not supposed to carry those burdens. He is not built to carry stress and worry because that it is not his job. During those tough times, God asks me to leave it all at His feet because He gave His *only* Son so I would not have to carry the burdens of man. He assured me that I needed to trust Him and just walk away from all that heaviness and never revisit them. He instructed through His scripture that worry was a burden for Him to carry and since it would not add one day onto my life, there was no need for me to engage in it. He taught me how to count all things as joy and that joy is a gift He gives to us. Through my ever-growing trust in God, I have learned to be better. I have learned to be a better father, a better partner, a better friend and a better man. I am an eternal optimist, always trying to find a positive in every situation. That only comes through trust in God and the realization that He has each of us exactly where He wants us. Our steps are already ordered and it really is up to us to walk the path with Him or not. I choose to walk it with

Him and trust that He will be patient with me along the way. I thank Him for loving me, in spite of myself. My life has truly been a journey of adversity and blessings. I AM UNDERDOG!

## THE UNDERDOG PLEDGE

I AM UNDERDOG because today is the beginning of the rest of my life.  I will not be a prisoner to my past, but instead I will use it as a stepping stone to a brighter future.
I AM UNDERDOG because I believe in me and even in my darkest hour, I know without any doubt, that I am never alone.  I will overcome because I know that I can, and if I were you, I wouldn't bet against me!
I AM A WINNER!
I AM A SURVIVOR!
I AM UNDERDOG!

# Throwback NFL Cards

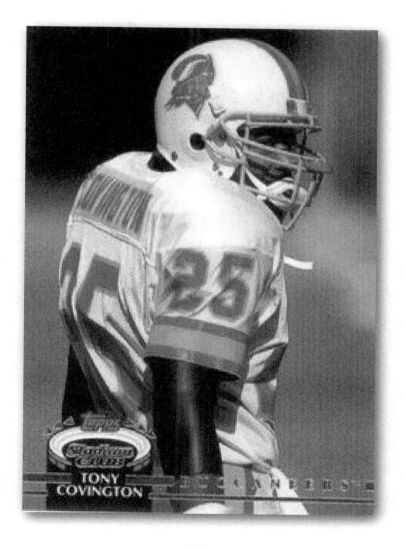

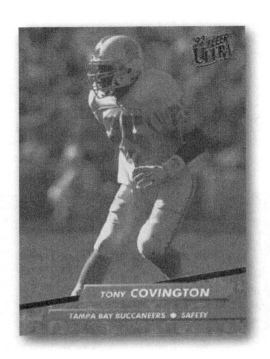

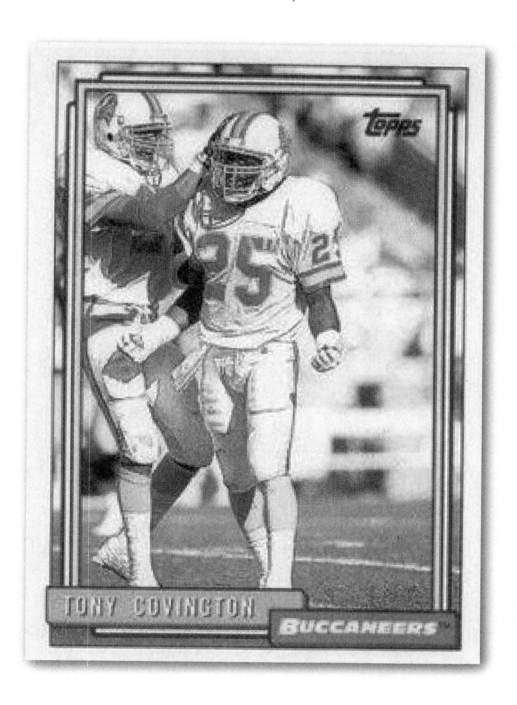

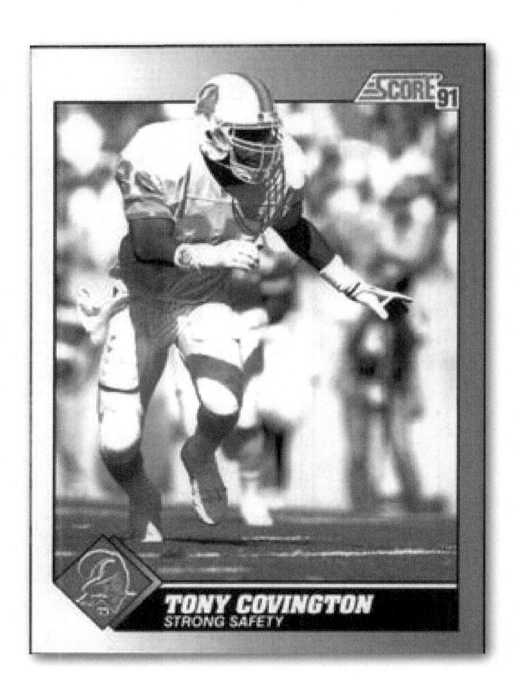

ALL ROOKIE TEAM

Tony Covington                    S

16. last
3. 14
42 last
2 7

Made in the USA
Middletown, DE
07 November 2021